SPROUTING HAPPINESS

THE 5 BRANCHES TO A
HAPPY AND BALANCED LIFE

JAMIE MACKENZIE

ISBN: 978-1-0683067-0-9

Cover and illustration design by: Neil Summerfield

FOR DAD

**WITH A SPECIAL
DEDICATION TO MY NAN
"MOPSIE"**

To my family

Happiness is a way of life.

Each of you have inspired my happiness.

Each of you have inspired my life.

Thank you for helping me embrace long-lasting happiness.

Contents

STORIES
CHANGE
LIVES

Introduction

It was a beautiful day in London. Sunny and warm, which for me meant navigating the hot network of underground tube trains to get to the event that I was attending. I was in my suit, which was too tight. This also meant that I faced my typical and inevitable moments of fiddling with the belt, trying to get comfortable and pulling my shirt out, trying to avoid the sweat marks seeping through.

I arrived at the venue and entered a very busy lobby, people everywhere. It was a large and low-ceilinged room which meant that the sounds of conversation and laughter were all around me. It also meant that the smells of coffee, tea and freshly baked pastries were unavoidable and drawing me into their location. I had arrived about 20 minutes earlier than my colleagues, and so after taking a coffee and a couple of pastries, I did what many people do when waiting in this type of scenario. I got out my phone and drifted off into a wormhole of digital information and content. Before I knew it, I felt a tap on my shoulder and sure enough, a couple of my colleagues had arrived.

Given the nature of the event - a very public one - there were a couple of photographers going around and capturing candid pictures of people mingling together. Personally, I prefer these types of shots, the natural ones that capture the authentic you, rather than the posed and polished pictures we all try to perfect.

On this day, the photographers did their job so well that they captured more than just a person's hair colour, face, skin tone, or outfit. This picture revealed something much deeper, peering beyond the exterior to expose the truth of the feelings hidden within.

People talk about epiphany moments, a time when you suddenly feel that you understand, or you become conscious of something that is very important to you. It seems to be this intuitive grasp of reality through something which is both simple in nature, but extremely striking in its impact.

I had never experienced an epiphany until two weeks after this event.

A message popped up on my screen, and it was from one of my colleagues. They had forwarded me a link to the event website which we had attended. I will never forget the words which accompanied the link, which were "Jamie, you are famous". Overwhelmed with excitement and without hesitation, I clicked the link. Sure enough, up came the website for the event and, in turn, a series of pictures taken. The photographers had done a great job. I started to scroll down, scanning the images. "Where could I be?" I thought, and then I stopped.

I had found it.

In that moment, I held my breath and simply stared at the screen.

The phrase goes, "a picture paints a thousand words", and in this moment, the words that this picture was painting all led to a single destination.

Unhappiness.

This picture felt to me as though someone was holding up a mirror into my inner self. It offered a crystal-clear view of all the feelings, thoughts, and stories I had been telling myself for months while hiding them from everyone else. Yet now, it felt as though they were on full display to the world. In my inner turmoil and panic, I responded to my colleague, as I had to get instant feedback. Had they noticed what I could see? Could they see the unhappiness that was staring back at me?

So, I quickly typed back, "I have found it, not a fan of it. Wow, I look tired!" To my relief and amusement, they replied, "Don't be so hard on yourself, your tan looks good, and your facial hair is really coming along nicely ☺." In that moment I allowed myself a second to laugh, to let the brief hit of endorphins flow through my body, allowing myself to forget the issue at hand. But it didn't last long. My eyes immediately looked up, locking onto the picture.

After what seemed like hours of staring at the screen, I then, for the first time in my life, had an epiphany, and a negative one at that.

This moment of bleakness, whereby the only path ahead I could see was shrouded in unhappiness and dread, became the turning point. It was the moment I realised I had to act, to do something that so many people either overlook or avoid. I had ignored it, but I knew that I couldn't anymore, and now it was time to be courageous and make a choice. It was time to prioritise...

Sprouting Happiness.

I used to believe that happiness was about that dopamine hit, a quick shot of joy, instant gratification. These moments have their place. But are they lasting? With a quick high comes a quick low. Today I believe that true happiness, or as I call it, long-lasting happiness, is about that consistent everyday build. It is the continual stream of happiness inputs woven into what you do, why you are doing it and who you are doing it with. These small, progressive actions are what truly sprout your happiness. Of course, life will bring challenge, failure, sadness, frustration, loss, but when those moments come, you'll fall back on the bedrock of happiness you've built, a solid foundation that allows you to bounce back stronger every time.

This book, *Sprouting Happiness: The 5 Branches to a Happy and Balanced Life*, explores, through my own lived experiences and the inspiring stories of twenty-nine others, how I have made tangible, positive changes to my life. By grounding my actions in five branches that I have designed to focus on long-lasting happiness, I've experienced impacts I never could have imagined over the past sixteen months. However, these branches are not just for me, they are for anyone, at any stage of their life, including you.

In today's world, we often find ourselves swept up in the tides of the vast, choppy sea we call life. It's easy to let ourselves be carried along, but one thing we should never lose sight of is our happiness.

Happiness is there for all eight billion of us on this planet to find, nurture, and enjoy. *Sprouting Happiness – The 5 Branches to a Happy and Balanced Life*, I hope, will inspire you to reflect on your own happiness, make it a priority, and recognise the positive impact it can have on your life. When you are truly happy, your energy, aura, and output become infectious, not just for you, but for everyone around you.

So, let's make sure that happiness becomes your everyday.

HAPPINESS
IS FOR THE
EVERYDAY

HAPPINESS
IS A WAY OF LIFE

Part 1:

The Happiness Conundrum

In creating this book, alongside the journey I have been on in the last sixteen months, I have spoken to many different people about the topic of happiness. In all the conversations that I have had, there has been one question in particular which has had the same physical response from every single person. The type of reaction which sees someone demonstrate in front of your very own eyes that you have asked them a question which requires real deep reflection, and at times, internal conflict to give an answer. This question has always resulted in a person taking an intake of breath and a slight movement backwards:

"What is your perception of happiness?"

And there it is, the question which has really challenged everyone that I have spoken to. Not only does this question prompt people to reflect on their personal perception of happiness, but once answered, there is then a subconscious self-question that they then ask themselves, "Am I happy?"

In those few minutes, it seems they are truly looking at themselves. Some like the answers they give, and some not so much. However, everyone I have spoken to has given me an answer, and while there is a lot of variety, there is also a common theme which connects them all, including my own.

What is happiness?

There is no universally accepted definition of happiness, it is more a collection of elements which are linked. The *Oxford English Dictionary* defines it as, "the state of pleasurable contentment of mind; deep pleasure in or contentment with one's circumstances." The *Cambridge Dictionary* says, "the feeling of pleasure or satisfaction", and *Wikipedia* says, "a state of mind characterised by positive emotions, a sense of purpose, and a feeling of fulfilment." These more formalised definitions present two notions of consideration. The first is this immediate and in-the-moment feeling of pleasure, which could well be achieving something of importance, eating your favourite food, or being intimate with your lover. The second notion is centred on purpose and personal fulfilment, so you could say a longer-term, consistent and holistic outlook on your actions, environment, and choices. This is also backed by science, where there are two levels of identified happiness, one of instant excitement – hedonism - and one of longer term and stable contentment – eudaimonism.

Coming back to the question which I have asked those who have contributed to this book, "what is your perception of happiness?" these were some of the answers:

"When I have family and career in harmony."

"Knowing what's important to me and trying to achieve it."

"Happiness is what you decide, not what society tells you."

"When I am living in alignment."

"When I have aligned who I am with what I am doing."

"Being content in my life and finding joyful moments."

"Self-worth, sense of purpose and self-fulfilment."

"Being grateful for what you have in life."

"Permanent feeling of fulfilment."

I love this question, and I love these answers. The beauty is that we are now moving away from a traditional definition, and instead exploring what the feeling of happiness, truly means to people. For me this is incredibly powerful. The perception of happiness is individual to each person, and that is what makes it so special. When you say the word happiness, broadly speaking, we all know how that feels to us, what we then start to do is imagine, visualise and then articulate it.

Exploring this further, I spent some time with Matt Phelan. Matt is the co-founder of *The Happiness Index*, the author of *Workplace Happiness* and a TEDx speaker on the topic of happiness. When I asked Matt the question above he said, "Having access to thirty-seven million data points across four million people in over one-hundred and seventy countries, the more I learn about happiness, the less I feel I know! It's very hard to define it universally, but every single day we learn more about what drives it. My broad definition of workplace happiness would be, "Subjective wellbeing at work". To be even more specific, I define employee engagement as what we think about work and employee happiness as what we feel about work."

There is no one universal definition of happiness, and there shouldn't be. This deep routed feeling is not just individual to each of us, but also incredibly important. From the reflections shared by the many people whom I have engaged with on this book, it is quite clear to me that on paper the definition is not universal and is blurred. However, definitions aside, when you say the word happiness, the feelings and the articulation of what it means to people while individual, are very similar. It is centred on longer-term fulfilment, purpose, creating, and living in an environment which is truly aligned to who you are and what you want.

Reflection moment

Take a few seconds to pause.

What comes to your mind when I ask for your perception of happiness? Be brave and honest in your reflection.

Note it down for your own reference. We can get tied up in technicalities sometimes and lose sight of what that feeling of happiness really means to us, and only you know the answer to it.

The science behind happiness

Having explored what the definition and perception of happiness is, and how people feel about it, all of which is, well, subjective, it is important therefore not to ignore the science behind it. To understand more, bring more context and to balance the topic of happiness with objectivity, I had the pleasure of speaking with Clive Hyland, author, speaker, and thought leader on the topic of Neuroscience. Clive was kind enough to share his reflections and answer my questions, to help us understand more.

Neuroscience and happiness interview with Clive Hyland

How do we know that the brain is linked to our happiness?
This has been evidenced through the roles of both psychology and neuroscience. Psychology centres around the understanding of the mind through the observation of behaviours and exploration of the subjective human experience. Neuroscience focusses on what is

activated inside the brain (typically using image and technology) during different experiences, such as stress or indeed happiness.

How does science approach happiness?

There are two types of happiness. The first is what I refer to as high arousal happiness. This is something like excitement and must be temporary. Why? Because at this point, we are biologically out of balance with high doses of hormones in the body, such as dopamine, serotonin, adrenaline etc, which inevitably must come down. This is exacerbated in states of falsely induced happiness enabled by drugs. The comedown must happen. This is where depression can kick in, and even addiction.

That said, these immediate hits of happiness which occur, providing they are not detrimental to our health, should be enjoyed as part of our life.

The second type of happiness is what I refer to as low arousal happiness, which is where we drop back into balance. This state has many names such as contentment, peace, fulfilment, calmness. It is our anchor or baseline state, differing from states of excitement because it is sustainable and not susceptible to the highs and lows. In biological terms, this is referred to as a state of homeostasis, a maintenance state, much like a car just ticking over.

In an ideal world, we would live life enjoying the peaks and highs of happiness, but more importantly, our baseline state of long-lasting happiness would be at a higher level so that we never drop too far down. That would be, scientifically, the perfect balance of happiness.

How does the brain directly impact our happiness?

Our brains create neural pathways, which then drive our actions. In most instances we don't know our brains well enough to be able to understand the interactions between our thoughts and emotions, and if we aren't careful, we can be hijacked by them, which in turn will impact our happiness through our decisions and actions. If we look at how long it takes for key moments to happen in our brain, then this is what the first half a second looks like:

Instincts / Emotions 0.08 sec	Rational Thought 0.25 sec	Reflection 0.42 sec

In our day-to-day lives, many of our responses are based on our emotions, and this is vitally important as emotions enable us to connect. However, thought enables us to take in more information to make informed choices, decisions and free ourselves from the emotional and instinctive high. Being reflective is when we have much more conscious thought, more imagination, can look beyond the immediate experience and more so, this moment is also where we have the ability to change.

Why is this information important? Because a lot of people's problems today, which impact their happiness, exist because they don't sufficiently understand their brain-body intelligence system and how it works. In a world where we are challenged with global threat, experience personal anxiety, and are presented with more information than what the brain can handle, we should understand how our brain works so that we can use time more effectively to better manage our reactions and decisions.

What can people take away from the science of happiness?

As humans we are much more emotionally centric than we have previously recognised. Why? Because we have highly sensitive systems throughout our brains and body which enable us to sense our immediate environment and what's going on around us.

So, it really is about being more aware about what is happening in your body and your brain at a particular moment in time. For example, as soon as you feel yourself tensing up inside, a peak of adrenaline, then a great first step is to get better at noticing that. Once you have, take a bit more time to use the reflective part of your brain and start the process of better understanding what is happening. Ask yourself, why are you getting so emotionally charged by something? Remember, it only takes 0.42 seconds.

Taking time, both in and post the moment, will allow your thoughts and reflections to process the emotion that you are experiencing and in turn help you to handle the situation, moderate your emotions and make more considered decisions and actions. This approach will allow you to raise the baseline of your balanced state of long-lasting happiness and limit the risk of in-balance and emotional hijacking.

Finally, what neuroscience tells us is that brain health is of the utmost importance in sustaining a productive and happy life, and this is directly influenced by your emotions. So, taking time to understand your emotional history and behaviours gives you a much better chance of reaching a higher baseline in your balanced state of long-lasting happiness, and the healthier your brain will be.

Until this point I had never realised just how much of a connection the brain, and our body has with our happiness. By understanding more about how neuroscience and physiology work together, it can improve the self-awareness of how we can control it to make a more positive impact.

The importance of happiness

I have a task for you. Ready?

Whether it be the short, pleasurable, and arousal-filled happiness, or the constant and consistent long-lasting happiness, I would like you think about a life without happiness. Take two minutes, time it, and just think about it...

Welcome back. How was it?

I can't imagine that the life you were thinking about is one that you would want to spend a great deal of time in. In fact, it could well be a life that you would do everything in your power to avoid. Yet, how many times a day do you proactively think about your happiness?

How much of what you do each day contributes to your happiness? How aligned is your everyday life to your happiness?

When in a place of long-lasting happiness, magic can happen. The quality of our decisions and actions is so much higher, not just positively impacting us directly, but also those around us. When you are the best version of yourself, you give the best version of yourself, and when you give the best version of yourself, you get the best back.

Happiness also has a direct impact and benefit on our individual wellbeing. It leads to improved mental health, reduced stress, anxiety, and feelings of depression. Likewise, the physical impacts include stronger immune systems and lower blood pressure. It fosters a more positive mindset, improved relationships and develops our personal resilience in coping with challenges and setbacks.

Whilst happiness is important, when you are living at a hundred miles an hour, darting between life's tasks and pressures, it is easy to forget.

Never, ever, forget.

At this early stage of the book, I felt it incredibly important to explore perspective and provide context of what happiness means, both subjectively and through a more scientific lens. In the past I have been confused about what happiness is, asking myself the questions, is it the pursuit? Is it the destination? Is it about the people? Is it looking good in a mirror? Is it earning lots of money? Am I happy?

Today I have a greater sense of clarity and understanding about happiness, and I hope that now you have too. This has allowed me to experience and write about sprouting happiness through the lens of the everyday, that long-lasting balance which exists as the baseline of our happiness. My focus is not to fill it with short bursts of highs to mask the baseline. My focus has been to raise the baseline so that when I do enjoy the highs, the comedown is a step and not a fall.

This is what the "happiness" in *Sprouting Happiness,* is all about.

Key reflection

We have explored the happiness conundrum, tackling head-on its varied definition and the science behind it, including both its high and low arousals. We also recognised the importance of happiness, and why we should proactively take the time to focus on it.

Takeaways

- Whilst there is no universal definition of happiness, the perception and feeling are that it is centred around living a life aligned to who you are.

- The science tells us that we need balance in happiness. A combination of hormonal peaks complemented by a consistently high everyday baseline.

- Taking time to proactively focus on creating and living long-lasting happiness will have a positive impact on our individual, and collective wellbeing.

Sprouting happiness reflections

We all have our own individual relationship with happiness, whether it be finding it, nurturing it, improving it, or even changing it. Take a moment to reflect and note down the following:

Why is sprouting happiness important to you?

Where can a focus on happiness make a difference for you?

IT STARTS WITH YOU

Part 2:

Reflections in the Mirror

When was the last time you looked in the mirror? Ok, I don't mean when you were brushing your teeth, washing your hands, sorting out your bed hair, or applying your makeup. I mean when did you last stand there, seeing past the material and the cosmetics, your eyes firmly fixed on the reflection of the person looking back at you.

I pulled up to the house at 9pm, after a 4-hour drive back from the office. I still had that picture which the photographer had taken, imprinted in my mind. Instead of shaking it from my memory, I was hyper-focusing on it, remembering all the tiny details. The emptiness in my eyes, a posture lacking energy, a shirt and buttons struggling to hold themselves together, and a look that conveyed not just a sense of being lost, but that I didn't seem to care.

.

Like most days, I walked through the front door and gave my wife a hug and a kiss, and she asked me, "How was your day?" I replied, "It was good thanks honey."

I hadn't been truthful with my wife.

I walked upstairs, a walk that for some reason, seemed to take a lot longer than normal. I threw my bag down to the floor and felt a desperation to simply strip myself down, out of my "office attire", an escape, maybe so that I could disassociate myself from what was imprinted in my mind. It didn't work. However, in that moment, I did something which normally I would never do. My typical routine would be to grab my PJs, to get comfy, to get out of a work mindset. Instead, I decided to walk to the full-length mirror in the corner of the room and stood there.

If I could overlay this moment with music, without question it would be to the song *Man in the Mirror* by Michael Jackson. If you haven't heard it before, give it a listen, but more so, listen to the words. Standing there, stripped bare, I looked long and hard at the man in the mirror, and I asked myself the question, what do I see?

Internally, I was now fighting an avalanche of emotion, expression and reflective thoughts that if I wasn't careful would spin me out of control. What came to me first was a man who professionally was lost, disengaged, lacking confidence and belief in his ability. Next came a man who was being served with a feast of time with people who were negative and destructive, and in parallel being starved of time with the people who made the biggest and most positive difference in his life. This was followed by a man whose inner self was lost, fading, disconnected from the physical being and no longer in control. Then came a man who physically had terrible eating habits, lacked any real movement, energy, and was putting strain on his body. Finally, I saw a man who was no longer the author of his story, subservient to other authors, allowing them to write the content, the chapters, and to edit out the parts which meant the most.

In a moment of pure vulnerability, I had self-reflected on the man in the mirror, and with tears rolling down my face, I knew that it was time to make a change.

This wasn't just about changing jobs. The trigger for this moment in my life came from the picture taken of me at the event which had a profound impact on me. It was the window into me that I needed. But it wasn't solely about the job, it was more about the fact that I had allowed myself to lose the balance, to lose the control across several areas. I had lost agency in my story, and my baseline of long-lasting happiness was dropping.

Reflecting on this moment, I can see now that my mindset was overrun with the bad, the negative, all the things which were dragging me down. This is very common and is a psychological phenomenon known as negativity bias. This evolved from early humans as a survival mechanism which prioritises threat and danger in our environments. We all have it in us, and in this moment it had me pinned down. This is not to say that I didn't have good and positive things in my life which were promoting my happiness. Of course I did (and do today), however, in that moment, I simply could not see them.

It starts with you

At this point, I wasn't looking to blame anyone, I wasn't looking for a scapegoat, and I certainly wasn't looking for excuses. Instead, my mind went searching for solutions, racing to figure out how I could do something about all these thoughts that were flying around in my head. As each solution came to me, so did a single common denominator which was integral for all of them. It was the one thing that was needed if I was going to do something about how I was feeling.

I grabbed my PJs, put them on and as I walked towards the bedroom door, I turned my head and looked for a final time, staring at the man in the mirror, and what was looking back at me was the one thing that I needed in order to make a change.

Me.

As I walked down the stairs, I knew that if I was going to do something about how I was feeling, take back control, grab the pen and be the author of my story and my long-lasting happiness, then it had to start with me.

Now this wasn't about trying to do it all myself, far from it. I need people to help me, advise, support, and validate. These are all important to me. If you aren't willing to recognise that the start begins with you, then not only will you not be able to move forward, but you also won't be able to accept and hold a helping hand.

I walked into the front room where my wife was sitting. I sat down next to her and simply said, "Honey, my day wasn't good." From there, I explained everything.

I was ready to be the start, and I was also ready for a helping hand.

Don't wait for the big moments

When I look back, I waited for a big moment, a major trigger in my life to prompt me into doing something about it. It was reactionary. One of my biggest learnings over the last sixteen months is that waiting for something to break before acting on it is not healthy. When I stood in front of that mirror, triggered by the picture I had seen of myself earlier in the day, I found it very easy to unpack the things that were wrong, and in some detail. These didn't just appear from nowhere, they had been building over time. I was subconsciously aware of them. I knew they were problems which were negatively impacting my long-lasting happiness, pulling down my baseline. So why did I wait for a breaking point to act on it?

This isn't uncommon. Dealing with challenging situations, feelings, moments, is not easy and I think it is natural for many to avoid, but this isn't healthy. Over the last sixteen months, I have learnt the importance of proactively getting on top of what I believe are the most important drivers of your long-lasting happiness. The constants in your life which will always be there in your everyday, the ones which feed and can raise your happiness baseline. Now, this doesn't mean that you completely avoid situations, moments, experiences which can negatively impact your happiness. What it does mean is that you can respond to them, and faster, because you are aware, you have a stronger foundation, and you are willing to tackle them.

Prioritising your happiness

We are all everyday people, living everyday lives, taking everyday opportunities and dealing with everyday challenges. Through my own experiences, with the insights of many others, this book addresses how you can proactively work on and prioritise your long-lasting happiness. Not to wait, like I did, for the dashboard lights to start flashing, but to continually monitor and continually act. Happiness is very real, and we deserve to live a life full of it.

So, are you ready to start sprouting your happiness?

Key reflection

I have shared a moment of major reflection with you by looking at the man in the mirror. Realising that the issues had been festering for a while, I knew I had to act, and that it had to start with me. We also recognised the importance of not waiting for something to break, but to be aware, get on top of it, and proactively prioritise your long-lasting happiness.

Takeaways

♦ Your baseline of long-lasting happiness can be impacted across several areas including your professional value, people, your inner self, the physical you, and your story.

♦ If you want to make a change, no matter how big or how small, then the change must start with you. Only then will you have the willingness to move forward and to accept the help of others.

♦ At times we can wait for something big to happen before we react, we let the elastic band stretch so much, even to the point of snapping before releasing the pressure. It is important to become more aware and get proactive so that you are in control of your baseline happiness.

Sprouting happiness reflections

We are about to prioritise and focus on sprouting our happiness. But before we do, ask yourself this:

Is the person in your mirror willing to be the start?

"WE ARE HAPPY WHEN WE ARE GROWING"

Part 3:

The Five Branches

Ok, so I made the decision that I had to start, to prioritise sprouting my happiness. Great, but now what?

I needed a way to focus on the key areas that would positively and directly impact my long-lasting happiness. More than that, I wanted a way of life, something sustainable, not just a quick fix for when things go wrong. Finally, I sought an approach that could be universally applicable, for everyone. Possible? Absolutely.

I believe that self-recognising and acknowledging that you want to make a change is incredibly hard. Then, taking accountability in making a start, requires tremendous courage. But what comes next, in the actions you take to make it happen, requires structure and support. This is why I wanted to create something that not only I could use to help me focus on the most impactful areas, but others could too. The question, "Now what?" at times, is a difficult one to answer, especially if it is you, and you alone, answering it.

So, let's answer it together.

Trees face ever-changing environments. To grow and thrive, they adapt, with their branches playing a vital role. Branches provide structure, carry nutrients, support growth, bear fruit, and help the tree make the most of its surroundings.

When I began this journey sixteen months ago, I realised I needed the same kind of structure, areas of focus, that could adapt with what was happening around me, whilst supporting the changes I had to make.

So, I created the five branches. Applicable to everyone, they positively impact happiness and are within our control through the choices and actions we take. Whilst we'll explore each in detail throughout this book, here's a brief introduction to them:

1. Story

We tell ourselves many things every day: who I am, where I am going, what is going to happen, how I will feel, who will be with me. We tell ourselves stories before they have even happened. Depending on the narrative of your story, which you have created, this has the power to either manifest itself into a positive pathway positive guiding you towards your long-lasting happiness or sabotage your efforts before you have even begun.

2. People

While we are individual in our being, we share our being with others. People are around us all the time and we form connections, build relationships, and expose ourselves to influence. Through our engagement with other people, we can experience friendship, support, kindness and love, but equally we can experience hostility, bullying, cruelty and hate. Exposure to people, and the nature of it, will have a direct impact on our long-lasting happiness.

3. Physical

Our body is our physical vessel through life, and it gives us the ability to live. Whether it be through movement, through what you consume, or through recovery, how we treat our body will determine how we feel and perform, and the performance of our body will directly impact our long-lasting happiness.

4. Inner Self

Looking inside our physical, I believe that we have our inner self, or what is best described in the context of this book, as the essence of who we are. Much like our body, our inner self also needs to be treated well, energised and connected. While the other four areas will contribute to this, a dedicated awareness and focus on our inner self will directly impact our long-lasting happiness.

5. Value

In the main, we need to create and trade our time in return for economic value, which is commonly known as money. This can come in many forms and represents a significant percentage of our daily life. Whether it's full-time, part-time, self-employment, unemployment, or retirement, the way we choose to spend our time and monetise our value directly impacts our long-lasting happiness.

Your life, how you live it, the decisions you make, and the actions you take are unique to you. My situation, which has driven my desire to focus on prioritising my long-lasting happiness will not be the same as yours. You may well relate strongly to your situation in life right now, but it won't be the same. What is the same though, and what does connect eight billion of us, is that we all go through times in our lives where our baseline of happiness is being impacted, good and bad. The specifics of how and the level of impact might be different, but the fact that it will happen is the same.

Focussing on these five branches will give you your "now what?" They will provide you with not just areas to work on in the immediate sense, but also every day into the future. As we explore these branches in more detail and their impact on our baseline of long-lasting happiness, we'll also see that, while each is individual, there are many crossovers. After all, happiness is fluid.

Five is more than just a number in this context. In fact, five can mean something even deeper. We will explore later in the book about the importance of numbers in the context of happiness, especially for me. But is it coincidence, chance, or even fate, that when I explored the meaning of the number five, what came back was an association with freedom, change, new possibilities and personal growth?

Maybe five is the new happiness number.

Final countdown

Our final countdown is here. Are you ready to prioritise sprouting your happiness? I am sure that already you are now thinking of how you can apply the five branches to where you are today and where you want to be tomorrow.

Am I right?

These are universal enough so that they can be adopted and applied at any moment by everyday people, in everyday lives, doing everyday things. I have been using these branches for the past sixteen months, and as you'll see, the positive impact on my baseline happiness has been significant. This is no longer a programme or a project for me, it is now everyday life, and I would urge you to think of it as the same.

The opportunity to improve the long-lasting happiness of people is literally limitless, and the benefits of doing so are worth the efforts.

When you are in a happy place - and what I mean here is at a baseline level - how much better is life? Our overall performance as a human being is better and the outcomes of that will be more positive. It could be increased confidence, improved cognitive function, reduced stress, a stronger immune system, greater creativity and efficiency, better communication, all of which have a positive knock-on effect, leading to even more positive outcomes.

Whatever lens or context you're reading this book through, the five branches are universal and can be applied to you. We all deserve to live a happy life, and more importantly, it is within our control to make it happen.

Key reflection

With the important question of "Now what?" we've been introduced to the five branches, which will positively impact your baseline level of long-lasting happiness. These branches are not just for moments of crisis, but for the everyday living of life.

Takeaways

♦ Once deciding to start, it is important to have an answer to "Now what?"

♦ I created the five branches so that they can be adopted at any moment, by everyday people, living everyday lives.

♦ They comprise of: story, people, physical, inner self and value, all of which directly and positively impact our baseline of long-lasting happiness.

Sprouting happiness reflections

With our five branches now firmly in your mind, you may well be already thinking about applying them. Take a moment to reflect on the following:

Which of the five resonate with you the most?

Where can you see the benefit of focussing on these?

Out of ten, where would you score your existing baseline level of long-lasting happiness?

WE CAN ALL BECOME AUTHORS OF OUR OWN HAPPINESS

1. Story

My eyes start to open, I move my body a little, cortisol and neurotransmitters are now being released, brainwaves start to change, blood pressure, heart and breathing rates increase, and as I sit up, I now realise that I am awake. With that comes the next phase. For me, this has always been inevitable and featuring every day since I can remember. Have you heard of *Jackanory*? It was a TV programme in the UK in which known personalities would read stories to the watching audience.

Upon waking, in my mind, *Jackanory* is on the TV, and the chosen story for today was the same story that was being read every day. My story. If you've read my first book, *28 Bags of Sprouts – Storytelling with Impact*, you will know that I am a great believer in the power of storytelling and stories. This is no different when it comes to the topic of happiness. I believe that we are living out the self-story which we tell ourselves every day, and this will influence and direct our choices, decisions and actions. So, what do I mean by this?...

I am sure that you have heard of 'imposter syndrome'. This is a persistent inability to self-believe that success is deserved or legitimately achieved. In other words, those with imposter syndrome see themselves as frauds and hold a fear of being found out, despite their achievements.

An example of this is when you gain a promotion at work and tell yourself, and even others, that it was simply due to luck. This is a self-story, and it can be dangerous. Telling yourself the story that any success you have is purely luck, not deserving and fraudulent, will create a lack of self-belief in yourself and, in turn, lead to wider issues, and have a detrimental impact on your happiness.

However, imagine if you were to view it differently. Recognising how your promotion came about, the training you did, hard work you put in, the level you performed at consistently, impact you had on others, and then use this to create a different self-story. What this then leads onto is self-confidence, self-belief, feel-good factor, and in turn, a more positive impact on your happiness.

Our self-story can lead and enable us to live a life of long-lasting happiness, but equally, if we are not careful and we are not tuned in, it can do the opposite.

Tuning in

It was the morning after the night before, where I had reflected on the picture I saw, and the man in the mirror. The alarm went off at 5am, my eyes opened and sure enough *Jackanory* was on the TV, and it started to play in my mind. But this day was different. This day I consciously listened to the story, I tuned in, and I didn't like what I was hearing.

"Today, Jamie, you will not perform as a person. You will not see your son before he wakes up and you will not see him before bedtime. Your clothes will feel too tight, you will have low energy and be out of breath when walking between office locations in London. You will continue to be disengaged in what you do, and when you do it, you will feel that you are doing it wrong. You will eat the wrong food to momentarily distract yourself and when you get home, you will be emotionally withdrawn. Finally, when you go to bed, you will have a restless night because you must do it all again tomorrow."

It is sometimes so much easier to ignore, rather than to deal with, and as the saying goes, "ignorance is bliss". But equally it isn't always just about ignoring, as there are times when you hear, but you don't listen. It's true isn't it. I do this sometimes with music. My wife will ask me if I like a song, I say yes, and she then asks if it is because of the words. My usual response is, "what words?" When you get familiar, into a rhythm, things become automatic, habitual, and for many situations and reasons, this is important. However, there are moments, like this, when sometimes you need to come off autopilot and listen.

For the first time, in a long time, I listened intently to the story playing out in my mind, I tuned in and realised that this story was not only unsustainable and detrimental to my long-lasting happiness, but that it had to change, and fast.

Reflection moment

When did you last tune into your story?

Take a few moments to reflect and listen to the self-story that you are telling yourself.

You are the author

Imagine being set the task of reading the story of your future. The catch, however, is that it has been written by someone else.

Are you the author of your story?

I had lost control and ownership of the pen; I was no longer writing my own story. Don't get me wrong, there were times when I willingly handed the pen to others for good reasons. But where I truly lost control was when I no longer held the pen. Either I allowed others to dictate the narrative, or they simply took it from me. Author and writing analogies aside, what I was experiencing in my day-to-day life was controlling me, not the other way round. I had lost not just the empowerment to shape my path, but also the self-confidence to do so. Recognising this was an important step for me. Why?

If you are to prioritise focussing on your long-lasting happiness, then you need the ability to be in control of writing your story. Only you can do this. Like any author, and I speak from experience, what you create comes from an idea, a vision, and you will gather insights, opinions, views, influences from others to help. But the key here is that they don't write the story, the author does, because it's the author who truly knows what it should be.

This is the same with your story. No one else can write it. After you have tuned into your current story, you now need to be able to grab the pen and make sure that you are the author. This doesn't mean that at this very stage you are starting to live it, what it means is that you are willing to pick up the pen. As we explored in part 2, reflections in the mirror, there is significance in accepting that it starts with you, when choosing to prioritise your happiness, nothing can happen unless you take the action. It is the same here. Your story can and will help you improve the baseline of your long-lasting happiness, but this can only happen if you, and you only, are willing to be not just an author, but a prolific one too.

Aligning your narrative

With pen in hand, it is now time to craft the all-important narrative. This is the path which connects everything, the spine that holds it all together, the direction of your story which every day will guide and keep your decisions and actions centred on prioritising the improvement of your long-lasting happiness. But where do you start with such an important step?

I was sitting at the kitchen table, my wife with me. In the few days that had passed since I shared how I was feeling, we had talked a lot about what it meant, and that I needed to change things. However, now we were at the point of getting started, and I needed a new narrative. Not easy when you are already feeling lost.

I talk more about people in the next chapter, however, the importance of my wife in this moment is significant. She was that safe and much-needed person who, whilst she wasn't in the weeds with me, knew me well enough to help me get out of them. However, it was the three questions which she asked me that were significant and enabled me to discover and create my narrative.

They were:

Jamie, what does living a happy and balanced life look like?

Jamie, what are you willing to do to live a happy and balanced life?

Jamie, what can you tell yourself every day to remind you of the importance of living a happy and balanced life?

Before we get into my answers, I want to recognise the courage and bravery of my wife in asking these questions. She had no idea what I was going to say, the nature of my answers, the Pandora's box which could well be opened. There's a tendency to avoid facing the tricky things that play out in our minds, preferring not to deal with them. However, in this moment, she was ready and willing to not just listen, but also support what was about to come. Thank you, Nicola.

So, what were the answers to the questions I hear you ask. The first, "What does living a happy and balanced life look like?" came naturally it seemed to me.

"Being present for my family. Having purpose and enjoyment in the work that I do. Being controllably healthy and physically confident. Having freedom to make the choices and take the actions which focus on my long-lasting happiness."

There is more behind each of these, which I explore within the other four branches, however these were what stood out to me. With them coming so naturally as they did, it suggested to me that I already knew what living a happy and balanced life looked like, which isn't always the case. I also want to point out here that there are no wrong answers. These were my answers, my reflections, and what I felt were right for me. Now these might not be the answers that you might give, that doesn't matter, because this is not about comparison, and never should be. Comparing yourself to others is natural, but dangerous, especially when it comes to reflecting on happiness. What is more important here is to tune into yourself and answering the question through your lens, and your lens only.

The next question, "What are you willing to do to live a happy and balanced life?" then shifted my mind towards making it happen. This was less about the how, but more about the willingness within me to act, and in my case, make changes. My answer to this came quickly and with a certain conviction in my voice.

"Anything."

In hindsight, I had left my situation late. I had waited for the big moment to happen before I acted. This is my context, my situation and unique to me. You might be reading this book as someone interested in taking your long-lasting happiness more seriously, you could already be living a happy and balanced life and are interested in how others approach it, or you could be feeling that you are losing balance, a dropping baseline of long-lasting happiness, maybe even rock bottom, and you want to do something about it. Whatever your context, your answer and the urgency within its tone will differ, but importantly, it will be right for you. My answer, its urgency, and scope of willingness was right for me, because I knew, that for this chapter of my narrative at least, I was ready to do "anything."

The final question that my wife asked me, I found very interesting. She knows me well, and in that she knows I need occasional reminders of why I am doing things, why I am making choices, why I am showing up. She also knew that the change I needed to go on was going to be hard, and therefore I would need these reminders, arguably more than ever. So, when she asked me, "What can you tell yourself every day to remind you of the importance of living a happy and balanced life?" I settled on

"Life is short, life comes once. Life living true to myself
is a life of long-lasting happiness".

In my answer came self-recognition, that the importance of this is linked back to being true to myself, in anything and everything that I do. Every challenge I faced, every change I embraced, and every moment of achievement or joy I experienced had to be a result of living true to myself.

That for me was the important link in sprouting my happiness. I believe that we all have the need for this, the need to remind ourselves as to why. Whether it be subtle and infrequent, or obvious and regular, that mental acknowledgement of the importance in what you do, can be the difference between acting or not.

In these three questions I had constructed my narrative. In front of me was the direction which I needed to help me start, make changes, and live out every day with a focus on happiness and balance. I had a clear view of what it would look like, what I was willing to do and the importance of it to me.

Reflection moment

Take a few moments to reflect on your narrative. Do you have one running through your mind? Is it aligned to where you are? How would you change it?

Chapters

If you were to go back 10 years, and I were to ask you the question, "What is your perception of long-lasting happiness?" would your answer be the same as today?

Chapters play a role in stories. They can be used to break the story into manageable sections, help pace it, focus on a particular event, or mark a transition or change in time. I believe that this is the same as we transition through our lives, and as a result, it allows our core story to venture into new areas. The key here is to be aware of that, and more so, be open to it.

If I go back to my twenties, it was a time when my perception of happiness was money, climbing a corporate career ladder, buying nice material objects and experiences, and I would make sacrifices at the time to live that happiness. My twenties were a different chapter of my story, and now fast-forwarding twenty years, this couldn't be any further from the chapter that I started sixteen months ago at the age of 42.

Looking back, and with the deeper reflections and understanding that I have now, I held onto closing chapters for too long and delayed starting new ones. This created friction in myself and led to a drop in the baseline of my long-lasting happiness, because I wasn't living the chapter that my story, and narrative, were aligned to. Did I think about it back then the way I do now? Absolutely not.

Later in the book, you will come across the chapter "Stories Change Lives", which is a collection of relatable insights on the topic of happiness from people who have played a part in my life. As you read it, think about this topic of chapters, they are recognised and noted more than you may be expecting.

Being open to new chapters in your story is one thing, recognising their impact on the baseline of your long-lasting happiness is another, but then being the author of them, writing them, and then turning the page to live them, is arguably the hardest. Be aware of the chapter that you are currently in, and if it is no longer aligned to your story, your narrative and your long lasting-happiness, then be open to turning the page and starting a new one.

Story time

When I reflect, to a point in time as far as I can remember, I have always had something which was guiding me. At school I was learning and growing, the purpose was to achieve the best grades that I could. At university it was the same (with alcohol and partying thrown in). In my twenties and beyond, it was about performing in my roles at work and exploring new relationships. My decisions and actions throughout this time were shaped by the guidance that either I had placed on myself, or that was placed on me by others. In hindsight, as time went on, I had allowed the control to shift to others and in turn what this meant was that the story time I was living, was not the story time I wanted, or that made me happy.

In having your own narrative established, no matter how big or how small, you will have the direction and guidance in place which you can use to help with those everyday decisions and actions that you take. It could be anything from:

Choosing fruit for breakfast or a bacon sandwich

Going for a 25-minute walk or staying inside

Reaching out for help or going it alone

Saying thank you or saying nothing at all

Having that difficult conversation or avoiding it

Hitting that "apply now" button or waiting until next time

Swiping right or swiping left

It isn't about which decisions and actions are the right ones or the wrong ones, it's more about ensuring that they are being taken in respect of their alignment to your story. If I were to apply my old narrative, which I touched on at the start of this chapter, to my decisions and actions today, then I would be living out a different life, and a life which would not be positively impacting my long-lasting happiness. However, today I am living within my new narrative, a new chapter, and while I am not a slave to it, I am in control of it, and I use it to guide and direct my decisions and actions every day. If what I do every day is within this context, then I know that my story time is the one that I want to live.

In many respects, this branch, "story", does become the overarching one, the lead one, you could call it, which can inspire decision and action in the other four, given that you are being guided by the narrative. As I mentioned earlier, while the branches have their own focus, they will also naturally connect, and you will see this as we continue to explore them in more detail.

Staying relevant

In life, nothing stands still, and this is the same when it comes to our first branch, "story". Situations will occur, factors will come into play, many are outside of our control and, well, things will change. Knowing this therefore, it is important that we stay relevant to our now. So, how do we do this?

We run our story not once, but on a cycle. We first tune in, and listen to the self-story playing out. If it is relevant, great, keep listening and living it, but if it isn't then it might be time to pick up the pen again and become the author. Align your narrative, the chapter that you are in, and then take the ownership to ensure that your story time is prioritising and making a positive impact on your long-lasting happiness.

Our self-stories are powerful. Being the author and incorporating them into your day-to-day life, at the level and depth which is appropriate to you, helps you focus on the decisions and actions that will contribute to you sprouting happiness and living a happy and balanced life, as defined by you.

Personally, I have found this the most important starting point in prioritising my long-lasting happiness. Every day I check in with myself, a constant reminder of my narrative and a constant reference in guiding me into considered decisions and actions. This doesn't mean that I plan everything or take ages to make a call on something, it just means that if something.

- ◆ Prevents me from being present for my family
- ◆ Doesn't give me purpose or enjoyment in my work
- ◆ Negatively impacts my health and physique
- ◆ Removes my freedom to make decisions and take actions in favour of my long-lasting happiness

Then, I won't be doing it. That is the importance I now place on my long-lasting happiness.

Key reflection

Ready to become a prolific author of your happiness story? Our first and arguably leading branch is centred on our self-stories. By recognising their influence on your decisions and actions, tuning in, and aligning your narrative and chapter, you can challenge your perspective and shift your focus toward positively impacting your long-lasting happiness.

Takeaways

♦ Stay tuned to your story, recognising when it is becoming detrimental to your long-lasting happiness.

♦ Be the author. Accept help, insights, reflections from others, however, always be in control of the pen.

♦ Align your narrative through three initial questions to one that is centred on what will improve your long-lasting happiness.

♦ Be aware of the chapter that you are in, they can and will change over time, the key is knowing when to turn the page.

♦ Live your story through your decisions and actions whilst not forgetting to stay relevant by checking in on yourself.

Sprouting happiness reflections

Is your self-story centred on your long-lasting happiness? Take a moment to reflect on the following:

What does living a happy and balanced life look like for you?

What are you willing to do to live it?

What can you tell yourself to remind you of its importance?

"NO ROAD IS LONG
WHEN YOU HAVE
GOOD COMPANY"

2. People

I stood there and looked up. I could see the two metal bars dead centre in my view, the grips on them ready for me to hold on and attempt what would be a major milestone: a pull-up. Just before I lifted my arms, I heard the shouts of "Jamie, wait, wait!" My brother Gavin and Harry, a personal trainer at the gym, were coming over. Stopping in their positions, both to record the attempt and to be with me in the moment, they looked at me and said, "You can do it." With two incredibly supportive people, who had been with me since the first day of my movement journey (more on that later), both looking on, I raised my arms aloft grasped the handles and inhaled a deep breath of oxygen. I then lifted. Feeling myself leave the floor, I was already in disbelief, this had never happened before, but as my muscles tensed, straining to lift the seventeen stone of bodyweight being pulled back down by gravity, I started to doubt, until I heard two voices.

"Come on Jamie, go, go, go."

In that moment, it felt as if they had their hands on my feet, and with all their strength, might, and energy they were working with me, wanting me to make it. All I could think of were the last 18 weeks of work, support, encouragement and collective desire to achieve.

Like a shot of indescribable power from within, my body responded. My arms and shoulders pulled me higher, my legs rose, my chin got closer and closer, until... I hit the top. As I lowered my body, feet touching the floor, I could hear cheering and clapping. I had done it, my first pull-up. Eighteen weeks prior I couldn't have even held my own bodyweight, let alone lift myself off the floor. But more than that, I had done it because of the encouragement, emotional support, collective desire, and human connection that I had from my brother who I have known for forty years, and a personal trainer who I never knew existed nineteen weeks before. Yet, they both played equal importance in a physical achievement that I thought would never be possible. My jubilation in this moment was one which I haven't felt for a long while, but this was amplified because of who was there, the journey leading up to it, and that we had lived this moment, together.

People are central to a happy and balanced life, which is why they form one of my five branches. People can ignite, transform, and grow the baseline of your long-lasting happiness; equally however, people can also negatively impact it, especially over a prolonged period. No matter how often you interact with people, their presence inevitably impacts you in many ways. The real question is: are these impacts contributing positively to your long-lasting happiness?

Reflection moment

Take a bird's eye view of the people you interact with on a regular basis, how are they impacting your long-lasting happiness?

It is your choice

I was presented with a unique opportunity at the end of September 2023. After ten years of working at the same company, I was leaving. When I joined the company in 2013, I had no say in who was already working there or who I would be interacting with during my time, whether I liked it or not, and for the most part, that factor remained unchanged. At the end of September, I now had a choice. Locally, the company employed approximately two hundred people, all of which I interacted with over the course of a year. Now, I engage with no more than ten, of which two are regular. I could have chosen to stay in touch with everyone, but I haven't.

You have a choice in who you surround yourself with, who you engage with, who you want to build connections, relationships, and trust with. We all have the power to choose, and in my experiences through life, you need to choose with wisdom and at times, courage.

I don't see this as being rude, non-inclusive, or disrespectful, it is about recognising people who will positively impact your long-lasting happiness, and then making the choice to be around them. However, what isn't right for you, doesn't mean that it isn't right for others. There are at times though when making a choice is driven by something more serious.

I'd like you to take a moment to reflect and think about someone you know who is surrounded by a toxic person or people. This person could be a friend, a colleague at work, a family member, or perhaps even you. You can evidently see that this toxic influence is having a direct and negative impact on them and their long-lasting happiness. Reflect on how they feel and what they might be going through. Now ask yourself, if you were empowered to make the choice to remove that toxic person or people from their lives, would you do it?

I know someone, and my answer to this question would be an unequivocable yes. However, that decision does not lay with me, it lays with them, and unfortunately, despite support, the mountain faced for them is too much to make that choice.

We all have a right to choose, and we are all empowered within ourselves to do so. Sometimes, the process is straightforward and simple; other times, it can be incredibly difficult and even carry significant risks to our safety. The key here, is that it is your choice.

Personally, I have made some incredibly difficult choices in my life, some of which have tested my emotional resilience, bravery and willingness to get through it, to the absolute limit. Equally, I have delayed choosing, or not made the choice at all, and I have learnt from that.

Choices aren't easy. sixteen months ago, I made a choice which would prioritise the people who I have intentional relationships with. These people proactively contribute to growing my long-lasting happiness. Those who don't, I have either removed from my life or have limited the number of interactions with, because I value and prioritise my happiness.

Setting your personal boundaries, in defining the people who you want to surround yourself can be hard, but necessary. These boundaries can cover many aspects including shared values, energy levels, kindness, gratitude, positivity and optimism, honesty, and respectfulness. While the list can be long, having the courage to establish it will allow you to set the boundaries which are there to protect your happiness. This will help to let go of the relationships which are detrimental to you but foster and even create the ones which will help you grow.

Never forget, long-lasting happiness is not about being surrounded by people; it is about being surrounded by the right people.

Reflection moment

With a focus on positively impacting your long-lasting happiness, note down the important boundaries which define who you surround yourself with?

Now ask yourself this, who is in and who is out?

Your inner circle

One of the most positive changes I have made is to actively recognise and curate my "inner circle." Now, this isn't a secret club located in the basement of my house, or an officially branded collective. This is a close-knit group of people who I can be my most vulnerable with. I lovingly refer to them as, "my team." This wasn't the case if I go back a few years. Yes, they were in my life, but circumstances were different, and I hadn't recognised the importance of an inner circle. So, what changed?

People came into my life, we got geographically closer, shared experiences, good and bad, suffered collective loss, navigated COVID and lockdown together and a lot more. When you experience with people the vast extremes that life can throw at you from the utopian highs through to the depths of sadness, you learn a lot about each other, and yourself. When it came to those moments in life, where I needed my most trusted, loyal and supportive people with me, they were there, always there.

These four people, my team, are my inner circle. They stood by my side sixteen months ago when I looked in the mirror and knew that I had to change, and they have stood by my side ever since. They know my story, hold me steady if I wobble, lift me if I fall, and inspire me to grow. They are a crucial part of my long-lasting happiness; I live to enjoy life with them both individually and collectively. But this works both ways, as whilst they are there for me, I am there for them, like all great teams should be.

Curating your inner circle, carefully choosing who you allow into your most personal and vulnerable spaces can be the difference between feeling supported, inspired, and growing your happiness, or feeling drained and directionless.

Reflection moment

Who would you consider to be in your inner circle? How do they contribute to your long-lasting happiness?

Meaningful connections

I believe that one of the most magical parts of being a human is having the ability to form deep emotional and meaningful connections with others. These connections don't just happen overnight, they require work to form and nurture over time, however when established they can play a key role in ensuring we have the right balance of relationship depth vs relationship quantity. Why is this important?

Making, and taking, the decision to step away from what has been a 20-year career has been one of the biggest in my life. I had been conditioned to rely on a predictable salary every month, to have people working alongside me, to follow a clear direction, and to operate within boundaries set by others. Now however, in every aspect of my life, I was experiencing the complete opposite. Whilst the prospect of writing my first book (*28 Bags of Sprouts: Storytelling with Impact*) and becoming self-employed was very exciting, I was filled with thoughts of fear, doubt, and a feeling of jeopardy. These haunted me most days, and even after the book launched in March 2024, becoming a top five bestseller in its category on Amazon, I was still plagued with these thoughts.

What helped me during this time were the depth of relationships and meaningful connections I had with certain people, and in certain areas, who I could talk to, share my feelings, be vulnerable with, and ask for advice and support. It helped me not just to mitigate those prominent thoughts, but also reduce feelings of stress, loneliness and isolation in the work that I was doing. In my case, going from working in an environment filled with people, to now working alone, was and is a huge shift.

So, what exactly is a meaningful connection, and how do we build one? It's highly subjective, and everyone has their own way of defining it. That said, there are three common elements: feeling seen, heard, and understood. Personally, I've found that the most meaningful connections are those where I can share how I'm truly feeling, knowing I'm being listened to and understood. These connections aren't limited to just one person. Over the past sixteen months, I've actively worked on cultivating deeper, more meaningful relationships with specific people in different areas of my life. These aren't necessarily the same people as before. Remember, in our 'Story' branch, we explored how narratives and chapters in our lives can change. In the same way, your needs evolve over time, and as a result, the people you build meaningful connections with will also change.

Recognising the importance of meaningful connections is one thing, identifying where and who you they can be built with is another, but building them will take time, effort and commitment. That said, their importance to your long-lasting happiness is significant. Having people with whom you can connect, share, express yourself, and receive emotional support and advice from will help you navigate the challenges, opportunities, and the highs and lows that life presents.

Reflection moment

What makes a personal connection meaningful for you?

Who would you like to develop a deeper connection with?

Communities

I walked through the door of the gym, past the small reception area and into an open warehouse style building. Around me was machine after machine, weight after weight, and muscles after muscles. I had never felt so out of place, that I didn't belong. My brother looked at me, recognising the mask of concern that I was wearing and said, "Don't worry, bro. This will feel like home soon enough." Do you know what? He was right. twenty-eight weeks on, I no longer have that feeling of not belonging, in fact it's quite the opposite. It's a space where I feel safe to connect with the team and other members, receive advice, learn, grow, share frustrations, celebrate achievements, offer support, and contribute. It is now a community that feels like a home, and more importantly, I know that I belong, and this has made such a positive difference to me and my long-lasting happiness (more on that later).

The human need to belong is a fundamental part of human nature and essential to our health, wellbeing and long-lasting happiness. Communities are where we find people and the opportunity to belong. They offer us the chance to set boundaries, choose who we surround ourselves with, and develop meaningful connections, social bonds, and interpersonal relationships. Communities can be found in many places. Some of the more familiar ones include family, friends, the workplace, health and wellness, hobbies or interests, cultural or ethnic groups, religious or spiritual circles, identity-based groups, online communities, and educational settings. The variety is vast, offering ample opportunity to explore areas that can positively contribute to our long-lasting happiness. Some of these will come into our lives through personal choice such as health, wellness or hobbies, some of these will come through necessity such as family, and some will be highly present and time consuming, such as the workplace.

Spotlight on workplace community

Since I started my very first job as a paperboy at the age of thirteen, I have experienced different workplace communities, which in the main have been extremely positive. At times, however, I have experienced some which have been extremely toxic. Having sat on the board of an employee engagement company for ten years, I have learnt the importance of engagement and happiness in the workplace. Not just because of the impact it can have on people while at work, but also because of the impact that it will have on people, outside of work. I have been in positions where the functional role I was employed to do, I was enjoying, however, the workplace community and culture that I was in, was having a negative and heavy impact on my long-lasting happiness.

I wanted to place a spotlight on the workplace here through the lens of people because I believe that it is one of the most prominent and impactful communities in our lives and if we aren't in tune with it, then it can and will have a detrimental impact on our happiness. Speaking on the topic with Matt Phelan, co-founder of *The Happiness Index* and *Employee Happiness* author, he said that "The data shows the four major drivers of happiness in the workplace are freedom, acknowledgement, (psychological) safety and positive relationships. These are the ingredients that need to be present in the workplace culture for happiness to thrive." Matt also went onto say, "There is a lack of knowledge around happiness, its importance in the workplace and the benefits which come from it. This ignorance is at every level in not understanding what happiness is, why it is important, how it leads to success, productivity, creativity, business outcomes, share prices etc. Happiness is wrongly seen as just the fluffy stuff; however, the data tells us otherwise and leaders in particular need more access to this information so that we can all understand more and act accordingly."

What I found interesting in what Matt talked about is that these are all related to impacts made by people, not necessarily the functional elements of the jobs that people are doing.

I also discussed this topic with Suzie Carr, Experienced Global Human Resources Officer. Suzie says, "Your workplace community is important, and can have a huge impact on your happiness, remembering that most of your time is spent there, especially if you work full time. If you are unhappy in the workplace then it tends to spill into other aspects of your life and can become extremely overwhelming. On the flip side, if your workplace is positively impacting your happiness, then it's a win for everyone, for the employee, their family, and their business, as happiness at work correlates to employee engagement and in turn, performance. Personally, I have had the fortune to work with some of the most talented people in the world, and from them I have learnt so much."

Reflecting on both Matt's and Suzie's comments and my own triggers for making the changes that I have done, I can relate to the importance that the workplace community played in my decisions and actions. Whether it be your peers, teams, bosses or other stakeholders in your workplace community, these people will have a big impact on your long-lasting happiness. The question is, in what way?

Reflection moment – workplace community

How present and important is the workplace community in your life? What is its impact on your long-lasting happiness? How would you change it?

Communities play a vital role in our lives, serving as the spaces where our daily interactions as human beings unfold. Within them, we find a sense of belonging, live out our values, and demonstrate behaviours that shape who we are. We form connections, bonds, networks, express emotions, offer and receive support, show kindness, gratitude, and respect. We fail, learn, grow, thrive, celebrate victories, share experiences, create lasting memories, have fun, laugh together, and so much more. While not every day can always guarantee positive outcomes, the right communities and people, aligned to your story, will provide the opportunity to lift, change, even transform your life and have such a positive impact on your long-lasting happiness. On the flip side, the wrong communities and people, can derail and destroy, so choose wisely.

Communication

My belief is that the single most important currency on this planet is not financial. This currency is what we transact in every single day with other human beings, it enables us to connect with each other, make an impact, and change lives. This most valuable currency is communication. Going back in time to the early days of primal societies, no communication between humans would mean no food, no way to alert against predators, no way to survive. Fast forward to the modern day, no communication would mean that we simply would not be able to connect with other people, full stop. However, it is not just about the act of communicating, it is about how you communicate and in turn, the impact that you can make.

Let me share a story with you about Brussels sprouts.

It was Christmas Eve 1998, and I was working in my local greengrocer. That day, everyone was in the market for a particular vegetable, Brussels sprouts, and they were flying off the shelves. Back and forth I went, grabbing more sprouts and filling them up until 5pm came and the shop closed for the day. Filled with curiosity, I counted the number of bags of sprouts that we had sold. Twenty-eight in total. Fast forward two years and during an interview for a job placement, I shared this story when asked what I was most proud of. This story was the reason that I got the job. Now the job wasn't Chief Sales Officer of Brussels Sprouts, it was a marketing assistant position, however, in sharing the story with the passion, enthusiasm and energy that I did, it made me stand out from all the other candidates. I had made an impact with my communication, and that made all the difference. Now, you might be asking yourself, what is the relevance of that story to the changes I have made in the last sixteen months? Well, this story inspired me to write my first book, which has played a very important part in my long-lasting happiness (more on that later).

What we communicate, how we communicate and who we communicate to, will dramatically impact our long-lasting happiness. We spend 80% of our waking day in communication with other people, which leads us to treating it as hygiene, a commodity. We can get complacent, and unintentional miscommunication creeps in. Yet, with every communication comes a magical opportunity to make an impact and to make a positive difference for yourself and for others. So, with that off my chest, here are my top three tips to improve the impact of your communications:

1. **Authenticity**: Communicate as you, not as someone else. People will connect and buy into you, the authentic you. and if you try to be someone that you aren't, you will lose trust. It's true, not everyone will like who you are, but that's ok, what is important is that who you communicate with can see you for who you are, authentically you.

2. **Energy**: People feed off energy, an invisible force which can instantly impact how people feel. Leverage your inner energy appropriately in your communications to create engagement, express and elicit emotion, even change the moods of who you are with. Trust me, people don't always remember what you said but will remember how you made them feel.

3. **Dance**: Think about communication, like a dance. At times you will lead, at times others will take the lead, sometimes its fluid and harmonious, other times its erratic and disjointed. But if you can stay present, actively listen, and respond, then your dancing skills will improve and the better the dance will become.

I take all my communications very seriously; I treat every interaction I have as a moment of magic which not only positively impact the baseline of my long-lasting happiness, but for others also. I have merely scratched the surface of this topic, however if you do want to learn more about communication impact and more so how a storytelling approach can help improve it, then check out my bestselling book, *28 Bags of Sprouts – Storytelling with Impact* (available on Amazon), it is a superpower worth unlocking within you.

Loss

My parents met in 1971. Mum was seventeen, Dad was nineteen, and it was one of those love at first sight moments. They were engaged within six months and in 1973 they were married. Through their life, they spent every day together. They never had much, but they had each other. They worked hard, created, supported and loved their family. Every decision they took, they took it together, every experience they had, they experienced it together, and every challenge or opportunity life threw at them, they faced it together. They were a team. Forty-eight years after they came into each other's lives, Dad was diagnosed with bowel cancer. At this stage, it wasn't terminal, and all efforts would be made to fight it, which they did together. Despite an initial all clear, the cancer came back within six months, and whilst together they tried to fight the cancer once more, this time sadly, it wasn't enough. Through this period, Mum was Dad's carer, never leaving his side, doing everything she could for him, whilst at the same time, watching her husband, soul mate, suffer and slowly slip away. Mum was at his bedside when he, aged sixty-six, eventually passed away. In that moment, everyone who knew Dad faced the reality of life without him. But for mum, the person whom she loved so deeply and had spent every day of her adult life with for the last forty-nine years, was now gone.

This is loss. Whilst mum has suffered loss in her life, including her parents and 3 of her sisters, including her twin, I know that the loss of Dad has cut the deepest and hit the hardest. Yet, whilst she grieved, she did not allow herself to sink. She found purpose in caring for Dad's mum and in her family. She took her time to acclimatise to life without Dad, those everyday moments which were always with two, but now were with one. Step by step she built back, and today, four years on, is ready to make another big step in relocating closer to us.

By Mum's own admission, she will never again live and share a day like she would have done if Dad was still alive, and that has a real impact on her happiness. This, she can't change. However, what Mum knows is that when the day comes, she will once again be back with Dad, but until then, she is making decisions, acting and living her life with the highest baseline of long-lasting happiness that she possibly can. I admire her, she is an inspiration to me and my family, and her mindset and resilience through it all, is truly incredible. I am so proud of you, Mum.

Death isn't the only form of loss in life. People can leave relationships, friendships, divorce, relocation. In researching and writing this book, I have heard stories of many types of loss, some of them, so incredibly unjust. However loss manifests itself, whatever the circumstance in which people can leave our lives, we will all face it at some point, this is guaranteed. What isn't guaranteed though is the level of impact it has on our long-lasting happiness, and how we respond. My biggest learning from Mum when it comes to loss is to appreciate what you have when you have it. Don't be scared to miss it when it's gone, but learn to live the best life you can without it.

Reflection moment

Have you experienced loss? With a focus on your long-lasting happiness, looking back, which one thing would you have done differently in how you responded to it?

People are what life is all about, and so it would wrong of me not to have it as one of my branches in living a happy and balanced life. With a focus on your long-lasting happiness, being selective about who you surround yourself with, finding belonging in safe and supportive communities and building meaningful connections, will help you to create an environment where you can learn, grow and thrive with the help of the people around you.

Key reflection

There are eight billion people on earth, so you can't avoid them! People play a prevalent role in day-to-day life, whether it be through family, friendships, work colleagues or wider communities. Who you are surrounded with, the connections you form and how you engage with them, will have a direct impact on your long-lasting happiness.

Takeaways

♦ You have a choice as to who you surround yourself with, so make sure you choose the right people for you.

♦ Create and curate your inner circle, a safe place where you can be vulnerable, share and get the support you need.

♦ Know where your meaningful connections exist and build on them. We all need to reach out sometimes.

♦ Communities are key to belonging and give you the space to interact with many, just ensure that they align to what you need.

♦ Communication is the currency between people. The greater the impact, the greater the outcome.

♦ We will all experience loss. Learning how to face, respond and live beyond it can help shape its impact on our happiness.

Sprouting happiness reflections

Considering all that has been covered in this chapter, what changes can you make to ensure that the people around you, are those who are positively impacting your long-lasting happiness?

"YOU ARE THE OUTPUT OF YOUR INPUT"

3. Physical

I was out of breath and sweating, and it had only been five minutes.

It was an April afternoon in the heart of spring, and that time of year where the sun comes out and the temperatures start to enter their mid-teens once again. It is this time of year that I am looking for that excuse to get the BBQ fired up again, and on this April day, I had found that opportunity. What comes with this is an invite for my family, or inner circle as I have already spoken about, to come over and spend time together, coupled with some usually slightly burnt food. Before the cooking started, and whilst enjoying the sun outside in the garden, my boys, ages five and eight, were kicking the football about, and after a couple of minutes were asking my brother and I to join them.

The first two minutes were great, running a little, passing the ball, trying to get past each other. The next two minutes, I was starting to feel out of breath. I felt myself becoming more static and letting the boys and my brother do more of the moving around. The last minute I started to pant more in my breathing, I could feel sweat building, a heaviness in every movement I was making. I stopped. After only five minutes I was out of breath, sweating, and I had to sit down.

This, I believe, has been one of the most significant moments in my life. Sitting on the chair, all I could hear were my boys, with a tone of disappointment begging me to continue playing with them, "Come on Daddy, please play with us." I explained that Daddy couldn't because I had hurt my leg a little, but I hadn't, I was just too embarrassed to tell them the truth - that Daddy was so overweight that he could no longer last five minutes of kicking a football around with his sons. My brother, supportive as always, encouraged the boys and the three of them carried on.

As the minutes ticked by, I watched on. I could see the fun, laughter, and enjoyment that my boys and my brother were having. In front of my eyes, memories were being made, and happiness was flowing through all of them, which was amazing to see. However, this was cut short by a feeling of sadness and realisation that had surfaced from deep within me... I was not part of that happiness, and it was for reasons which were completely in my control. I was preventing myself from experiencing these happy life moments with my boys and my brother, because my physical state was in a bad place, and this was all my own choosing.

In that moment, I told myself three simple, but impactful words: "I must change." The reality was that this wasn't the first warning sign. About six months prior to my reflection in the mirror moment, I had blood tests and scans which highlighted issues related to my weight, lack of sleep, lack of movement, poor diet and mental pressures. Despite this, I hadn't reacted to the news in the same way as I did on this sunny day in April. So, what was the difference in moving me to make a change?

My work, my mission, is centred on the importance of stories and storytelling, as I believe there is magical influence these can have on people. The relatability, the emotion, the connection, these can all have such an overwhelming impact to a point where people can be moved, even to change. This story, which I lived out there and then with my boys and my brother, was enough to move me to change, not a doctor sitting behind a desk using medical terminology, much of which I didn't understand.

I was moved to change, and change I have.

Not everyone has a choice when it comes to their physical state and people will be presented with physical challenges which cannot be prevented or reversed. Undoubtedly, these will have differing impacts on their long-lasting happiness. When my Dad was diagnosed with bowel cancer, which was not his choice, whilst he did his best to mitigate it, there is no hiding from the fact that this had a direct and negative impact on his long-lasting happiness.

Over the last few months, I have realised more than ever before in my life, how much of an impact your physical state has on your long-lasting happiness. Not least because without it, life wouldn't exist, but more so because it will determine how you feel and how you perform.

Now, let me be clear here, much like I am not a neuroscientist like Clive Hyland, I am also not a Health and Performance Specialist or a Body and Nutrition Coach. However, after forty-three years, I have now made changes across three areas, and the results have been significant, all of which have culminated in a positive shift in my long-lasting happiness which I could never have imagined. More on the details of that later.

So, what can we do to take greater care of our physical state?

Movement

I have always thought that if you wanted to be physically healthy and keep in shape, that it was about running, cycling, and going to the gym. Now, for many, including me in the past, these can seem like mountains, especially if your focus on physical health is only just beginning. Very few people want to take on a mountain, especially when your confidence is at a level of taking on a few steps, and so this can already make your starting point a difficult mental battle. What I have noticed though is that there is a shift of narrative away from "exercise", and towards "movement". Interesting.

We can recognise "exercise" as specific activity and hard work, yet "movement" is recognised as a more natural everyday occurrence, and it is these subtle differences which can play a part in how our mindset opens itself up to them. My brother didn't say to me, "Jamie you need to exercise hard every day" to improve your physical state, he said, "Jamie you need to start by moving more". Same message delivered differently, and while I had already found my inspiration, his words made it sound more achievable. Everything that we do is all about movement, and the more that we can get the right level of balance in our movement quantity, quality and intensity, the more positive the impact will be on our physical state.

Movement is beneficial for your cardiovascular health, muscle and bone strength, metabolism, weight management, energy levels, hormone regulation, stress reduction, improved sleep, cognitive function, mental and emotional well-being, and the list goes on. So why is it that when life gets tougher, the pressures mount, and time becomes more limited, movement often feels less important? Can you relate to that?"

I was interested to get insights from experts on the topic of movement, how to get started, keep going and the benefits it can have on our physical state and happiness. And so a few have been kind enough to give their time and words.

Nikky Ricks – Fitness Professional | IFBB Pro Bodybuilder

There are two aspects to the importance of movement. The first links to an old Arabic saying which is "May all your dreams, bar one, come true." The human condition is to have challenges in life, something to strive for, and so if we don't have this, then we can lose both direction and purpose. The second aspect on movement importance is the physical impacts such as the reduction in body fat percentage, gut efficiency, a better balance of hormones, improvement in energy levels, and mental health.

As a fitness professional, one of the big challenges I see when it comes to starting out, is that people don't like to feel uncomfortable. What is important here is that this is natural and inherent within us and is linked to our primal instincts. Our brains want to conserve energy, and this is why our first fifteen minutes of any movement, exercise, workout, is the hardest. Not everyone is the same, some people will want dive right in, like you have done, Jamie, however it is important to assess the limits and characteristics of people to ensure that we are starting out in the right way.

Trying new things and finding out what you enjoy doing is very important, you don't have to go to the gym, do weight training, strength and conditioning work or heavy cardio. Movement is more just that. Why not gardening? Walking is an underrated form of movement and exercise, if you are just a little bit unfit or overweight, and don't have any joint issues or heart conditions, I would say get out and start with a twenty-minute walk at a brisk pace.

Having a long-term goal, micro goals and milestones, will also help to get you started. It can be absolutely anything. Be flexible with your micro goals, write them down, journalise the progress, move them if you need and adjust as you go. Accountability is also key, and this is where my work is so important, I hold people to account on both goals and commitments. There is a saying which I share with everyone I work with, "Motivation will get you started, consistency will keep you going, and discipline that will get you to your destination". This is the key to making it work in the long-term.

Imogen Davis – Heptathlete | Team GB Olympic Prospect

One of the biggest things you can do is to find something that you can connect and resonate with, that makes you realise that movement and exercise is important for you. This then becomes your intrinsic motivation which will get you started and keep you going. Timing is also another factor, people will say there is never a right time to do something, but the reality is that there never will be, so it is about doing it right now.

Another important approach is to consider what you do as an integration into your lifestyle, the big and the small changes, helping you to create those habits and to not see it as a quick short-term fix. Choosing to park further away from where you work and walking the rest, moving more in the day, going on that run. But also, it's about making things easier to move, such as building a schedule around it. You need to create that environment where it becomes your every day.

Tony Eames – Founder of *Total Active Hub*

Movement is essential for our physical health and long-lasting happiness, however getting started isn't always easy – we know that 80% of New Year's resolutions fail by February, and only 9% of people stick with them for a full year. To gain the benefit from movement, the first thing you must do is to start somewhere, getting up off the couch and opening the front door already marks the first step. When it comes to movement, it is important that you don't follow others because no one is the same, so you must think about what it is that you enjoy doing.

Another tip is to create accountability, and there are two ways in which you can do that. The first is to schedule and book out time dedicated for it, and the second is to find a buddy, someone who you can move with and in turn hold each other to account. Celebrating your wins, no matter how big or how mall, is also very important. We are very good at talking about what isn't going well, or what we could have achieved, as opposed to recognising the progress we have made.

Setting realistic goals will help you to keep your movement up. It could be an overarching longer-term goal, then broken down into smaller shorter-term goals. Being flexible and adjusting them is also important. They are great as targets, but equally they should move based on how you are getting on.

Sabrina Oostburg – TN 2022 Olympic Weightlifting Champion

The first thing I always say when it comes to getting started with movement, is to reach out to someone to do it with as this will help with accountability. Secondly, motivation is key, if you feel a spark of motivation to move, whatever that may be, don't wait, just do it. I remember watching a CrossFit documentary and wanted to try it, so I did. This was me acting immediately when I felt motivated. When I started weightlifting, I did it because my best friend just so happened to be a junior national Olympic medallist. So, I started training with her, watching, learning, asking questions, and this really inspired me. If the gym isn't for you then do something outside, running for example. My mom started running with three other friends to lose weight and she convinced me to join her on her runs. That club has grown and now has over three hundred members running around California.

Finally, goals also remain an important factor in this movement journey. Set them, but also know that they will change as you progress. For me, originally I wanted to be strong, then to inspire others, and now I train to help me perform to the best of my abilities as a college athlete. Movement is worth the effort. There's a lot of science that shows the benefits to fitness, as well as the strong links to long-lasting happiness.

Reflection moment

How often do you move? If you were to make one change to improve the amount you move, what would that be?

Fuel

I have always had an inconsistent relationship with food and drink. By inconsistent I mean periods of time when I seem to be consuming the types of food which would be associated with "comfort" or "treats", and then realising I shouldn't be doing that, so I switch to periods of time where I consume foods which are related to "dieting" or going "alcohol free". You could say that it is a bit of an all or nothing approach, at both ends of the spectrum, as to what I am consuming. Looking back, these extremes also correlated with moments in my life, times of high pressure or sadness, enjoyment or comfort, even motivation or determination to lose weight. Does this sound familiar?

This consistently inconsistent peak and trough approach to food and drink was not good for me, and hadn't been for some time, however it is an easy cycle to fall into. I don't know about you, but when shopping for food and drink, whether it be in-store or online, it is easy, convenient and tempting to choose the items which aren't necessarily the healthiest, and while the packaging paints a happy picture, the impact it has on your physical state won't be.

For the first time - yes, the first time - in forty-three years, I took the decision to re-educate myself on the impact that food and drink has on our bodies and what I learnt, was more than I expected. Some of the documented impacts, both positive and negative, are as follows:

Positive

- Energy levels
- Nutrition absorption
- Brain function
- Muscle repair and growth
- Immune system support
- Mood regulation
- Digestive health

Negative

- Weight gain
- Chronic diseases
- Energy crashes
- Inflammation
- Poor digestion
- Mental health
- Immune response

Maybe I have been naïve, ignorant, even avoidant, however this deeper understanding of the importance of what goes into our bodies and its impact on us, provided me with new perspective. The 70/30 rule is often mentioned in that what you consume accounts for about 70% of the results in weight management and fitness, two of the most common physical health goals. Science does back this notion up, in that what you consume has a more significant impact than exercise alone, cited in a study by the *Journal of the Academy of Nutrition and Dietetics*.

From these learnings though, came a bigger understanding for me which arguably has resulted in the biggest shift in my mindset, moving me away from this inconsistent switch between feast or famine. This understanding is centred around the word, "diet".

I have always had a negative perception of the word diet, mainly because in my context, over the years, it has always been associated with restricting what I enjoy, shorter term interventions and more broadly, failed attempts to manage my weight. As you can imagine, when I hear the word, it doesn't create this positive association I need to have with what I consume. So, I changed it. Today, I view what I consume not as my diet, but as my fuel. Why is that you may ask?

Fuel to me is what is broken down to give your physical state what it needs for the journey ahead. Fuel isn't about periodic restrictions, or overindulgence, it is about consistency, balance, and appropriateness. It is about fuelling your every day with what your body needs for the route that you have planned for it. The question then comes as to which mix of fuel is right for you? If you put unleaded fuel in a diesel car, it won't work, or if you only charged your electric vehicle to 50%, it would stop at half its range. We need the right mix and amount of fuel for our physical state to perform. For me, this mindset shift has created a totally different relationship with food and drink. This doesn't mean that I no longer eat what many would consider as "bad foods", or that I no longer consume alcohol. What is does mean is that they are part of the right mix of fuel which works for me and the road that I am driving along, a road which is dedicated to long-lasting happiness.

I spoke with Nikky Ricks on the topic of fuel, and its impacts and importance on our physical state. Nikky first started on the importance of our gut, "70-80% of the immune system is housed in the gut making it the largest immune organ in the body. A well-balanced microbiota, (colonies of bacteria and protozoa, in your gut) will play a major role in keeping your immune system fighting fit and will also enable the body to drive off harmful bacteria and viruses.

Including within your fuel a mix of foods such as good quality lean protein, good fats, fruits, vegetables, whole grains and nuts, will provide a good variety of nutrients and fuel for your microbiota, especially those rich in prebiotics."

Nikky then talked about the importance of carbohydrates, which more recently have picked up a bit of a bad reputation, "Glycogen is converted to glucose in your bloodstream and is your body's preferred source of energy. Glycogen fuels the muscles, the brain and helps to maintain core body temperature, not having enough of it in your system can make you feel weak, tired and "fuzzy" minded. The carbohydrates that we eat are the primary source of this fuel, or rather the preferred source, secondary are fats, lastly and least preferable is protein. The challenge with carbohydrates today comes from the type and quantity that are included in our diet, especially those which are highly processed. So, the key is ensuring that you have the right mix of simple and complex carbohydrates to keep blood sugar levels stable. These can be obtained through eating a variety of wholegrains, vegetables, fruits, and organic dairy foods, all of which should be included in breakfast and regular meals throughout the day."

Nikky's reflections emphasised to me the importance of the connection between the fuel we consume, and our physical state. I also explored this with Harry Beech, Lifestyle Personal Trainer and Mental Health Specialist. In talking to Harry, he recognised the importance of mentality, and its links to happiness, when it comes to relationships with food. "When you use foods to compensate for negative impacts happening in your life, like comfort eating, this then creates a negative association, which over time can lead you down a difficult and dark path, resulting in various mental health issues. You can be "happy" eating the wrong food, but it is important to know that this is short-term. By changing your mentality towards food and seeing it as positive "fuel" for your body and mind, this can avoid the attachment disorder and allow you to get in control and make better and more nutritional choices. This will result in not just physical, but also mental benefits too, not least boosting your energy and confidence."

Nikky and Harry's reflections, coupled with my own journey of re-education, has been an important reminder of the impact that food and drink can have on our physical state. However, it isn't easy to know what to do, especially in a world of growing choice, convenience and processed fast food.

Reflection moment

How do you feel about the balance of food and drink that you consume? If you could make one improvement, what would that be?

Recovery

It was late, about 10pm on a Thursday night, and I was staring down an empty motorway, on my way back home. It had been a busy week, and one that had included a lot of early morning and evening driving, around six hours a day. I had the music turned up, the air-conditioning was down to sixteen degrees Celsius, and my seat was positioned more upright that normal. I knew that I felt tired, both physically and mentally, but I still had another fifty miles to go. Close enough to keep going, I thought.

It seemed to happen quite quickly. I remember closing my eyes to blink, however, the reopening of them obviously took longer that I had expected. The next thing I could hear were the loud vibrations of the tyres touching the rumble strips at the edge of the motorway. My eyes opened, quickly, immediately alert and hands firmly on the wheel. I corrected the car, regained control, and took the next turning to find a suitable place to stop. Fortunately, the road was empty and as I was already in the left-hand lane, I had only drifted a few inches, however I had clearly drifted off to sleep, even momentarily. This is the first time it has happened to me, and it will be the last.

Our bodies demand sleep, and while they can't force you to eat when you are hungry, they can put you to sleep when your tiredness becomes too much, even when you are driving. My body clearly had been pushed too far and had not received the required levels of sleep that it needed. It really can be the difference between life and death. Sleep is by far the most important aspect of our physical recovery, and during its different stages, the body performs recovery functions. According to *The Sleep Foundation*, *The American Heart Association* and *The Cleveland Clinic*, the key stages and activities include:

- **NREM Stage 1 & 2:** Lighter sleep stages initiating recovery by relaxing muscles, slowing breathing and preparing the body for deeper sleep.

- **NREM Stage 3 (Deep sleep):** Allows for growth hormone release, physical tissue repair and growth, bolstering of the immune system, and removal of information your brain doesn't need.

- **REM Sleep:** Allows for mental recovery and restoration, memory consolidation, processing emotions, enhancing learning and the re-energising of your brain.

Research from the *National Sleep Foundation* reveals that chronic sleep deprivation can increase stress hormone levels, impair cognitive function, and reduce overall happiness by 39%. There's a reason people say, "There is nothing like a good night's sleep".

Recovery isn't just about getting enough sleep. Depending on what we put our bodies through, we might need more than forty winks. A holistic recovery routine can include practices like mindfulness, hydration, stretching, and balanced nutrition. Just as we explored the importance of fuelling ourselves for the journeys we undertake, the same principles apply to recovery. It's essential to:

1. **Sleep well:** Adults need seven-nine hours per night for optimal functioning.

2. **Stay hydrated**: Aim for three litres of water daily, increasing with physical activity.

3. **Fuel appropriately**: Align the fuel you are consuming with the demands of your activity levels.

4. **Rest your mind**: Practice mental recovery techniques like mindfulness or relaxation.

Recovery is about more than simply catching up on sleep, it's about recharging every part of your physical state. By consistently prioritising a balance of sleep, hydration, nutrition, and mental rest, aligned to what we need, allows us to recover well. In doing this, we don't just feel better physically, but also mentally, and in turn this will positively impact our long-lasting happiness.

Reflection moment

Do you recover well? Looking back on your last three days, how much sleep have you had? If it is less than seven hours per night, what changes could you make help get closer to that number?

My journey - physical change and its impact

I wanted to play football with my boys.

On 3rd June 2024, I sat down with my brother Gavin and explained how I needed to use that moment of sadness as motivation to make the biggest change I have experienced physically in my life. I spoke with my brother not just because I trust him with my feelings, but also because he has been dedicated to fitness and physical performance for his whole life. It plays a huge part in his mental wellbeing and his long-lasting happiness. I knew that I needed him to not just provide me with the right approach to making physical changes enabled by movement, fuel and recovery, but also to be by my side through it all. While I had the motivation to make the first step to change, I lacked confidence in doing it on my own, and so by having my brother with me, it would provide that encouragement, support and collective accountability, that I would so desperately need.

The plan

My brother was great in helping me explore and understand exactly what I wanted to achieve, the changes I was willing to make and the time I was willing to commit to the programme. What this resulted in was an overarching plan which gave me structure and focus, but also flexibility as I would progress through each week. The plan outlined the following:

1. An initial programme of 28-weeks
2. Identified goals for the end of the programme
3. A weekly rhythm of physical movement
4. A new mix of fuel
5. The recommended target for sleep recovery and hydration

The goals

Given the motivation for this change, my main goal was to be able to play football with my boys for as long as they did. However, as I mentioned in an earlier chapter, I wasn't happy with how I looked, what I was eating and how I felt on a day-to-day basis, so I also wanted to use this motivation to make wider changes to my physical state. In the end, while we were open to tracking other measures, we settled on two main goals;

1. A waist reduction of ten inches
2. An average strength increase of 150%

The movement

An important part of my movement plan was that I needed to enjoy it, as I knew that this would help me in ensuring that this change was permanent and not a one-off. We decided that the gym would become the staple part of my movement plan, giving me access to the needed equipment for strength and conditioning work, targeting a one-hour workout at lunchtime, up to five days a week, rotating on a cycle of different muscle groups (push, pull and legs). On top of this, and to support cardiovascular work, we added to the week three fitness sessions at thirty minutes each. This would start as walking, but when ready, would then move to other activities such as spin, football, and boxing fitness.

The fuel and recovery

With this change, I really wanted it to be of a new balance and lifestyle mindset, and not that of a diet for a set period. As I mentioned earlier, it is about the right mix of fuel that I needed to support the physical activity I would undergo every day. So, we changed everything. I incorporated a blend of foods, including eggs, sourdough, fruit, vegetables, fibre, wholemeal pasta and rice, and protein-based meats. I also included what we could class as treats. This was important to me as I never wanted to feel that I had to restrict or even remove certain food and drink. This was a lifestyle change after all. Applying a disciplined structure in when I was fuelling myself was another key change, ensuring that I was eating at breakfast, lunch and dinner as well as having snacks as needed in between. Finally, I had to work towards a hydration of four-five litres of water a day and a minimum of seven hours of sleep.

The journey

I remember doing my first shop; it was the Sunday before day one of the programme. I made sure I had all the right foods I needed to fuel myself correctly as per the plan. I also remember that it added about 40% to our weekly family shop cost - who said eating healthy was cheap? In picking up my brother on day one, my new training partner, I had already baked in accountability, and I was ready for it.

Walking into the gym, *War Machines* in Ramsgate, whilst I felt fully supported under my brother's guidance, I also felt very nervous and out of place. Unfamiliar surroundings, new faces, equipment I had no idea how to use. However, these were just barriers in my mind, which I quickly let go of as we settled into our exercises. By the end of that first week, I was more comfortable, and after meeting more people, I already started to feel part of the community.

Five weeks into the programme, I was already feeling major benefits. I had an established routine, habits had formed, and my motivation had now turned into consistency. I could see physical changes already. My posture and form were improving, and I was getting stronger. Within me, I had more energy, and my mental focus and clarity had improved significantly. To add to this positivity, I had the results of my first measurements. I had lost five inches off my waist and my strength was up 142%. I felt amazing.

At just over one month in, this can often be a crossroads moment: the point where motivation either transforms into consistency, routine, and habits, or fades away. For me, experiencing the benefits, successes, and positive feelings at this stage was incredibly important to keep me going.

Over the next few weeks, I remained committed and consistent, even as frustrations began to build. Progress seemed to slow, and when my brother injured himself and was sidelined for 4 weeks, it could have been easy to pull back. But I didn't. The supportive and encouraging community around me kept me motivated. By week twenty, I had achieved an eight-inch waist reduction, and an average strength increase of 256%.

"This was no longer a programme." These were the words I said to my brother when he asked what I would be doing after the twenty-eight weeks were up. This was now part of my life, and the movement, fuel and recovery I was doing was now etched into my daily discipline. On the 20th December 2024, my final measurements were in:

- I have lost ten inches off my waist
- My average strength is up by 302%
- I have lost fourteen pounds in weight
- My resting heart rate has reduced by 10 bpm
- I can play a full match of competitive football

I have hit my goals. But more than that, I have turned a moment of sadness into something that has changed my life forever. Today I am writing this as a stronger, fitter and healthier person. My physical state is in a place that it has never been before and the impact it has had on my mood, energy, confidence, wellbeing, mental state is immeasurable positive. But more than that, the impact that this has had on my long-lasting happiness is incomprehensible.

What made the difference

Reflecting on my twenty-eight week journey, I have focussed on the three key elements of the physical branch as explored in this chapter. Whilst it has been intense in terms of my schedule, I have ten key learnings that I believe are applicable to anyone either starting out on, or wanting to change their physical journey:

1. **Jump on your motivation**: My boys motivated me. If you have found a motivator, then don't hesitate to use it while its burning, it will propel you.

2. **Have support around you**: I had my brother and *War Machines*. Whether it be a buddy to move with, or a community to become part of, that additional support and accountability will help you throughout the journey.

3. **Find what you enjoy**: I found the gym. Incorporating what you enjoy, even passionate about, into the physical changes will keep you engaged through the good days and the bad days.

4. **Set goals**: I established two clear goals. Create longer-term goals for yourself and track your progress, however on a shorter-term level, have created goals and milestones which you can be flexible with.

5. **Create routine**: I scheduled lunchtime and early mornings. Ensuring that your routine is built around your day-to-day life, allows you to dedicate, but also respect other commitments you will have, and before you know it, you will have developed new habits.

6. **Celebrate the wins**: I wasn't afraid to share my progress. With every positive change you see, celebrate it, share it with the people around you, and be proud. This is a time to focus

on the positives and self-recognition for the hard work you are putting in.

7. **Setbacks are OK**: I was training on my own and felt progress frustration. You will suffer setbacks, injuries, a missed movement session. That's totally OK and is part of the journey. Just make sure that when you feel it, share it with others, as the support around you will help.

8. **Track and journal**: I kept a weekly journal of reflection for reference. This helps you to not just note your progress objectively, but also remind yourself of how you felt during the good and the difficult times.

9. **The little things matter**: Not one big thing made the difference for me, it was everything. Doing all the little things like leaving your trainers at the front door, or going to bed thirty minutes earlier, will help you to be the change you want to be.

10. **Motivation > consistency > discipline**: For me, this was a lifestyle change vs a quick fix. Baking movement, fuel and recovery into your day-to-day life, no matter how big or how small, will make a positive difference. Viewing it as a life change will help you to normalise as opposed to something with an expiry date.

Reflecting on this journey, it's clear to me that this wasn't just about playing football with my boys, it was about reclaiming my life. I've learned that physical health is more than just how you look; it's about how you feel, how you live, and the energy you bring to every moment. My physical transformation has been life-changing, but its real value lies in how it has sprouted my long-lasting happiness across every part of my being: my confidence, my relationships, and my ability to enjoy life fully.

If there's one message I'd leave you with, it's this: your physical branch is the foundation upon which so much of your happiness rests. It doesn't matter where you start, what matters is that you do start, and you keep going.

Key reflection

Your physical state enables you to live life fully, do what you love, and interact with the world around you. As such, it has a direct and high impact on your long-lasting happiness and therefore, it is essential not to neglect it. Providing your body with the right balance of movement, fuel and recovery will help it perform at its best.

Takeaways

♦ Move. Physical movement of any kind has profound impact on your health and body. Start small find what you enjoy and build a rhythm and routine that works for you.

♦ Ensure that you have the right mix of fuel going into your body, meeting its needs for nutrition, energy and recovery purposes.

♦ Prioritise recovery. Your body and mind need rest every day, so provide it with the right levels of sleep, hydration and mental relaxation.

♦ Embed your physical journey into your lifestyle. Create routines, build habits, engage with communities, and enjoyment in your activities. This will help you form a new, positive relationship with your physical self and enjoy the abundance of benefits that it will bring.

Sprouting happiness reflections

How could you change your approach to moving, fuelling and recovering your body to improve your overall wellbeing? What small changes could you make to create a lasting impact on your health and long-lasting happiness?

"IT'S TIME TO GIVE YOURSELF THE HUG THAT YOU WOULD GIVE TO OTHERS"

4. Inner Self

I was four weeks into writing. In my mind, I was on a timer, racing to complete the entirety of my first book as fast as possible. For every day that had passed, it seemed as though I was working later and later, skipping more breaks, and at times, food. I was totally blinkered and focussed on the end goal. I could feel myself getting more and more anxious, uptight, frustrated that time was running out. The reality though, was that it wasn't. My obsession to do things as fast as possible was counterproductive. and I was doing what I have done for a long time, which was head down, not stopping and just doing. On top of that, I was being incredibly critical of my work, doubting, judging, and self-sabotaging.

I know that many of these behaviours were born of legacy, circumstance and a strong feeling of imposter syndrome, nevertheless, they were present and destructive. Whilst I had taken the decision to make changes, aligned to my new chapter and narrative, I was doing the same as before, however this time, it was on a different project.

It was around 10.30pm, I turned my laptop off and walked downstairs. Noticing that my wife had gone to bed, I walked over to the kitchen sink to grab a drink. Reaching for a glass I noticed in the corner of my eye a note sitting on the side. The purple ink and style of writing told me it was from my wife, and as I stepped in closer, expecting to read something along the lines of, "Put the bins out", instead it read this:

"Don't forget to be kind to your inner self."

In the melee of all the change I was driving with courage, intent, conviction, and enthusiasm, I had forgotten the most important person of all.

Me.

My wife was right. Of all the good changes I was making to positively impact my long-lasting happiness, I was starting to forget the person who was driving everything, the inner Jamie, or what some people might call, the soul. This was an important reminder that whilst I was working on changes in my life such as the people around me, my job, exercise, diet, to have balance and longevity in my long-lasting happiness, I also needed to work on my inner self. It was now time to not just hug others, but to also hug myself.

Decluttering the mind

I lifted my wrist and looked at my watch. Selecting the heart-shaped symbol, I could see the number increasing. My heart rate was going up. Whilst physically I was stationary sitting in my chair, in my mind my thoughts were running at 100mph. Deciding to explore self-employment, write a book, and make big changes in my life all at once, was scary, and on this Wednesday morning in November it decided to remind me of that.

Thoughts were running through my mind, exploring all the things which could go wrong; that the book would be a failure, I would become unemployable, no-one would see value in what I did, that I would not be able to support my family. These thoughts were, on this Wednesday morning, trying their very best to sabotage and derail what I was doing. My anxiety was now ramping up, and so was my heart rate, and I could no longer be present and focus my energy on the task at hand, writing my book. Instead, my mind was cluttered with thoughts, concerns, worry, and an overwhelming sense of negativity. Anxiety was the thief stealing the present moment.

I recognised that I had to do something. I needed a change of scenery, somewhere that I could sit, regulate, reflect, and try to deal with what was cluttering my mind. The beach. One of the many blessings in my life is that I live very close to the beach, a beach which has played a big part in my younger years, and somewhere which I adore. After arriving, pen and notepad in hand, I found a spot just up from where the water was breaking, sat down, looked out to sea and just breathed. After about five minutes, the combination of the smell of the sea air, sound of the seagulls overhead and breaking waves close to my feet, had taken my focus away from the clutter. The result, my mind was emptying, and I had mentally, through the power of the environment around me, managed to get under control. However, it didn't stop there.

With (it felt like) a much clearer and decluttered mind, and surrounded by an environment which was clearly helping me, I picked up the pen and notepad and started to write. Taking advantage of the calmness of the situation and my renewed mental focus, I summarised the negative thoughts that I had on the left-hand page, picking off each one at a time. I then on the right-hand page, challenged myself to objectify and evidence them.

The result? I couldn't.

There was nothing that could substantiate the future that my thoughts were trying to predict. As I stood up, I brushed the sand off my jeans and looked down at my watch. My heart rate was now back to normal, and with that I took a deep breath and headed back home, ready to live for today.

This whole episode, from sitting in my chair through to having completed an assessment of my negative thoughts, took an hour, yet it was one of the most valuable learning experiences that I have had for such a long time. I had used self-awareness, taken action to regulate, immersed myself in nature to my advantage, journaled thoughts, and challenged myself rationally. Decluttering wasn't easy, but necessary, and given that I am the only one living in my mind, I was the only one who could truly understand where I needed to declutter. By doing so, it allowed me to gain clarity in my thinking and re-focus myself on doing the things which I was in control of, the things which were going to positively impact my long-lasting happiness.

Given that we are exposed to such an incredible amount of information every single day, bombarded with data from every angle, exposed to opinion, influence and a habit of comparison, it is of no surprise therefore that our minds can get cluttered and overwhelmed. If we are unable to manage this, allow the negative emotions to creep in, then it will have a detrimental impact on our minds and our long-lasting happiness. With a hunger to understand more about the importance of decluttering the mind, in what is a cluttered world, I spoke with experienced holistic health and wellbeing coach, Debbie Evans.

Mindfulness interview with Debbie Evans

What is mindfulness?

Mindfulness is simply the open acceptance of everything in the present moment. You can't turn off your brain from thinking, but you can eventually create space where you allow these thoughts to pass like clouds, witnessing but not reacting.

How can we go about de-cluttering the mind?

De-cluttering the mind can feel like opening a box of frogs! Everything pops up at once, but a good place to start is to check in with yourself and simply become aware of how you are feeling. Often, we "believe" our thoughts to be the absolute truth, but they aren't. Observing our thoughts and feelings from a place of stillness can help you to answer this question, "Is this true? Or am I just feeling." When we become aware of how our thoughts feel in our bodies, we begin to understand what the messages are that we need to hear and learn. Our minds can become saturated with worry. Anxiety is worrying about the future, depression is worrying about the past, but the reality is that you can't change any of it. You can't go backwards, you can't go forward, you can only be in your now, and this is where the change needs to be.

What can a de-cluttered mind show us?

Gaining clarity in the mind can expose the truthful thoughts, the parts of you which need addressing. This can be scary but necessary, as it prevents you from trapping yourself and it allows you to accept yourself truthfully. Self-awareness and self-acceptance are tools you can use to begin to unlearn the mistruths you have come to believe over time. Understanding that shame and guilt perhaps translate to self-forgiveness and self-love. Or the anxiety you are feeling about a situation, could be opportunity to look again, to gain clarity and understanding about the messages that your emotions are telling you.

Can our minds play tricks on us?

Our brains are set to negative bias, we're hard-wired biologically to be alert to danger, and anything that might cause us harm, our brains can't tell the difference between being chased by a dinosaur or that our drive to work was stressful. When you understand that your thoughts are not always true, you can change them. Letting go of the stories of "I'm not good enough" or "this always happens to me" and replacing those thoughts with "I understand that I am feeling this way, let me explore why" can bring clarity, reduce anxiety and fear, and allow your mind to come to a place of stillness. Reducing all the overwhelming noise means that you can truly choose what you wish to focus on next. Allowing you to spend your energy focusing on decisions and actions that will positively impact your long-lasting happiness.

What other practices can support clearing the mind?

As a student of yoga and mindfulness meditation, for the last twenty-five years, I have learnt that these practices work. When I find myself overwhelmed, the mantra "get out of your head and into your body" plays on a loop. Breathwork and mediation are great ways to create a "pause" in your mind to help you to find space in between your thoughts and emotions. When we are overwhelmed by whatever emotion or feeling we are experiencing we become disconnected from our bodies. Using yoga, or other movement, even something as simple as mindful walking, can reconnect us with ourselves. We process emotions when we move our bodies which helps to clear the pathways to return to sense of inner calm and equilibrium, a greater sense of balance in both our body and mind. Whatever you choose and however you move, being grounded back into your body will give you a clearer mind and a more positive outlook. Helping you to focus on your long-lasting happiness.

Reflection moment

Is your mind regularly cluttered? In moments where you feel overwhelmed, or have negative thoughts, what do you do to help declutter the mind?

Your inner guide

I really can't explain it, rationally at least. Since taking the decision sixteen months ago to proactively make changes and focus on my long-lasting happiness, whilst it has been incredibly scary, unknown and uncertain, it has also felt a natural path to take. I don't mean that focusing on happiness has surprised me. I mean as in the steps I am taking, decisions I am making and what I can visualise as the outcomes of what I am doing, all of it just feels right. More than ever, I am listening to myself, and my inner guide.

Before my Dad passed away, I asked him to look out for me, protect me, but more importantly, step in when he needed to and help guide me. A big part of me believes that when I need guidance and truly listen to myself, what many might call a gut feeling, the guidance

I receive often feels like it's coming from my Dad. This is something which I have never felt prior to my Dad passing. Whether it is or not, I will never know, but what it does give me is a feeling of assurance, confidence, and safety that the path I am now walking is the right path for me. This deeper level of trust that I am now developing with myself, my inner guide, I can say is positively contributing to my long-lasting happiness.

I do recognise that within this lies a spiritual context, which is very new for me. Numbers for example have meaning and can be markers for the path you are on. The number twenty-eight started my new professional journey, with my first book *28 Bags of Sprouts*, and it represents spectacular new starts, connecting with others, living in the moment and personal growth. Whether there is a deeper meaning to it I don't know, that said, I do take comfort in its seemingly close alignment to my recent change in journey direction.

In the spirit (excuse the pun) of this book being about exploring the different ways in which I have proactively focussed on my long-lasting happiness, I spent some time with John, a spiritualist, to understand more on the connection between belief, guidance and happiness. John says, "The spiritual context is all about help. Family plays such an important part in our happiness, as family is core to spiritual connections, and so in my beliefs, when they do pass, there is an opportunity to remain connected and supported by them. The bond is so strong that your family and loved ones will never go away, they are still willing and wanting to help and guide you. Those who believe in this will come to me, and I can try to share the information of support and help, from their loved ones, with them."

John also recognised those who would be more sceptical of the spiritual context, "Whilst there are a lot of people who don't believe in the spiritual side, they themselves will have a belief of their own where they would go to for help, it could be their living family or religious community. The key message is that, whatever your belief, help is there, and you don't have to be alone."

I was interested in John's reflection on loneliness, and wanted to understand a little more, "Being alone, thinking that you are on your own, I feel is where unhappiness can come from. No one to help, no one to support and guide, not being able to think straight, not being able to move forward. When you are in a low place, you are in a low place, and at times you can't think straight and it's only when you start speaking to someone else, that you start to get out of it. That's why talking to someone, whoever that is, is the key. Trusting in what you believe in, to help you get through what you need to get through, is important and a positive thing."

John's reflections highlighted two things for me: belief and guidance. In many respects, this comes back to my newly found inner guide. I listen to myself every day, and I believe in the guidance that I am taking ownership for, wherever it comes from.

Whatever your belief is, wherever your inner guidance is emanating from, it is important to listen to it and not feel alone or misaligned in your decisions and actions. You know yourself better than anyone else, and if you trust and believe in yourself to be your guide, then the path you walk, will be the one that is right for you.

Gratitude

I used to take things for granted, and typically it was the things which meant the most to me. It was only recently that I have become more aware of being grateful for what I have, something which is called gratitude. I am not a practitioner in gratitude; however, I do now recognise and appreciate more than ever what is important in my life. I find this an important part of keeping myself mentally grounded, balanced, and prevent a constantly moving bar of expectations in my mind getting out of control. If you are always wanting for more, you will lose sight of what you have.

Regularly, I will take a moment to think about and be thankful for the family I have, the connections I have created, the people who are supporting me, and that I am able to walk my son to school. I appreciate that I have technology enabling me to be creative, express my ideas, add value, and of course write books, that I am physically able to move, and that I live so close to the sea. I have found that these grounding reminders, help me to mitigate negative emotions, and to feel happier. This isn't to say that I wasn't grateful for what I had. The difference is that I am now actively aware of it, recognise it, and use the positive feeling and emotions it creates to impact my long-lasting happiness.

Gratitude and its link to happiness came up in a conversation I had with Niraj Kapur, LinkedIn Top Voice and Managing Director. Niraj was very open about how gratitude plays a key part in his happiness, "I used to wake up in the morning, be grateful for thirty-forty seconds and then get on with my day. However, I read about the importance of gratitude and of flooding your brain with positive emotions, which I now actively practice. So now I pray twice a day as opposed to once, I bought myself a standing desk for £130, which gives me so much energy in the afternoon. Again, I am so grateful I can afford this. I am grateful for the light that comes into my office, I am grateful for the technology I use, the fact I have a notepad and pen, and that I can afford multivitamin tablets."

With such a focus on this, I was keen to understand the impact that this has had on Niraj, "The impact of this practice is that I am just so grateful, and I am literally in a state of gratitude all day long. This makes a huge difference in how I talk to people, how I feel and more so, in how I now never compare myself to others, which for me is one of the greatest sources of unhappiness."

Recognising and practicing gratitude isn't new, and Niraj and I will not be the only people doing it. No doubt in reading this, you will be grateful for what you have in life, the question is, do you actively recognise it, remind yourself of it, and use it to positively impact your mind, emotional state, and long-lasting happiness.

Reflection moment

When was the last time you reflected on what you are thankful for? Take a moment to note down three things which you truly appreciate, and how they make you feel.

Nourishing your soul

Sometimes, just sometimes, the flame which burns inside of you needs a little oxygen, and in moments like this, you need to nourish your soul. Hard as it can be to objectify, nourishing your soul, through my lens, is doing the things which just make you feel connected and whole. It could be listening to a song, watching the sunset, sitting in nature, painting, drawing, and in these moments, space is created within you to get lost, relax, energise and to nourish the soul. Have you ever found yourself doing something and referring to it as therapeutic? My wife and I do this when we suddenly find ourselves joining our son in colouring in a picture.

Finding the time for these moments is important, as flames can go out. Personally, I love going for a walk along a stretch of cliff top near where I live, with headphones in listening to my favourite music. Also, when I write and am struggling for inspiration, I listen to music aligned to the tone and mood of which I am writing about, allowing me to reconnect with myself and my soul. With eight billion people on this planet, there are eight billion souls to be nourished and so with such individuality, only you will know what works for you. The key is that you do it. Taking the time to nourish the soul is not about being self-indulgent, it is about recognising and spending time doing the things which will positively impact your personal wellbeing, and your long-lasting happiness.

Reflection moment

How do you like to nourish your soul? Make a commitment to yourself to do one of those activities within the next week.

If you hurt yourself physically, you know it, most of the time you can see it, and when that happens, you will find a remedy to address it. The challenge with your inner self is that it is harder to see and know when its hurt, and therefore easier to forget. Much like you care for your physical self, it is very important to be kind and care for your inner self. This isn't about a single act, once in a blue moon, it is about a continual and proactive routine.

As humans, we love to give ourselves a great big kick, but rarely we give ourselves the hug that we would give to others. Working to mitigate the negativity which can exist in our minds, opening ourselves up to support and direction from those we love, being grateful for what we have as opposed to comparing ourselves to others, and taking time to allow ourselves to get lost in the moment, will all help to give our inner self the love it deserves. For me, focussing on this branch of inner self has been very new, yet until recently, I never appreciated its importance and impact.

They call it, "mind, body and soul" for a reason, and much like we have already explored with the body, by recognising and nourishing all three with equal importance, there will be a positive impact on your long-lasting happiness.

Key reflection

Our fourth branch, your inner self, is hidden away and can be easily forgotten, however much like the kindness you give to others, it is equally important to be kind to your inner self. Working to have clarity of mind, a trust in how you are guided and being grateful for what is around you will help to mitigate negativity and nurture a healthy inner flame.

Takeaways

♦ Taking care of the mind and decluttering it of negativity, will make more room for focus, clarity of thought and positivity.

♦ Developing and connecting with your inner guide that you both believe and can trust, will help you through the good times and the difficult times.

♦ Expressing gratitude for what you have, as opposed to comparing with others, will bring a greater level of appreciation.

♦ Being in nature, listening to music, reading, expression, whatever nourishes your soul, make sure that you incorporate it into your life so to keep that internal flame burning.

Sprouting happiness reflections

Have you been neglecting your inner self?

Building on this branch, note down three things that you can do, which will show kindness to your inner self. Then commit to yourself to doing them on a regular basis.

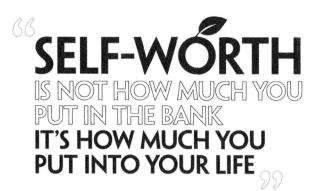

"SELF-WORTH
IS NOT HOW MUCH YOU
PUT IN THE BANK
IT'S HOW MUCH YOU
PUT INTO YOUR LIFE"

5. Value

It was a Friday, the end of my first week after leaving my previous company, and of course, it was the first week of my new chapter. I had decided to use the time to get myself organised before jumping into writing my new book. For a change of scenery, I was in a local coffee shop working on my laptop, when a lady tapped me on my shoulder and asked if she could sit opposite me. "Of course," I said.

She placed her handbag on the chair, sat down, and proceeded to open the sachet of sugar, pouring it into the cup in front of her. After stirring her coffee for a few seconds, she looked up at me and said, "Hi I'm Sue, what's your name?". Quite the normal question to ask someone when meeting them for the first time, so, I answered with pride and confidence, "I'm Jamie, lovely to meet you Sue". It was what happened next however, that I did not expect.

Sue replied, "Jamie, what a lovely name", and then followed up with a question which sent me into absolute internal chaos,

"What do you do for a job?"

Please challenge me on this, but isn't it the case that whenever you meet someone for the first time, you are always asked what you do for a job? It seems to be this instant test, and the resulting answer defines who you are as a person, how successful you are, and seemingly now branded from that point in the eyes of the audience.

So, what did I answer? In this state of panic and confusion as what I would tell Sue, who I had known for about twenty seconds, I simply replied, "I am not sure yet." For the first time since I can remember, I couldn't articulate what I did. But this for me, in that moment, meant so much more. I had lost my identity, it was as though everything I had done in my life for the last forty-two years was worthless, purely because I couldn't answer the question.

As I left that coffee shop, reflecting on my conversation with Sue, I realised something. Throughout my working career, which is a significant part of our lives, I had allowed the jobs I was in to define who I am and what my value was. Whereas, it should have been the other way around, in that who I am and the value I offer, should define what I do. Me as a person is what defines me, the values I hold dear, the purpose that I strive for, the skills that I have grown, the difference I want to make and the impact I can have.

I have been with my sister-in-law when someone asks her what she does, and her reply, sometimes apologetic in tone, "I am just a waitress". I find this hard to listen to. By letting the perception of the job define her, she is devaluing herself. The reality is that she isn't "just a waitress", she is an energetic, diligent, people-focussed, kind, compassionate and generous person. Ironically, these traits that don't always exist in some of the most highly paid and senior leaders in the workplace today.

As I've come to realise, finding real value in work doesn't mean defining ourselves by a job title; it means engaging in our work with intention, continually investing in our growth, connecting meaningfully, balancing priorities, and embracing the courage to make changes when needed. These are the building blocks of a fulfilling career which contributes to our happiness.

We create value, we convert that value into work, which we then convert into income, so that we can live. This takes up a significant part of our waking day and therefore, has a huge impact on us. It is so important therefore, that when we are asked the question, "What do you do?" that the answer we give is one which comes from a place which positively impacts your long-lasting happiness.

Purposeful engagement

What a contrast.

Upon deciding to write my very first book, I had identified six contributors whom I felt would add a great deal of value to the readers, much like I have done with this book. One of the contributors was Simon Alexander Ong, international keynote speaker, award-winning coach, and bestselling author of *Energize*. Simon had played a key role in igniting my desire of re-engaging and re-discovering what I wanted to do. During my interview with Simon, he asked me a question, "Why did you do the job you did?" I explained the context and that the why had changed over time, but in the end, I was doing it for the money. He then asked me, "Why do you do what you do now?", and my answer was very different.

Unrehearsed, what I said next came naturally, as if it was an unfiltered, authentic, and emotional response that came from my inner self. I said,

"Because I want to positively impact people of all ages through the power of storytelling."

In two simple questions, Simon had initiated a self-reflection within me that had made something so abundantly clear. It seemed impossible to me that two months prior, my engagement and happiness in a work context, had completely disappeared, yet on this day, two months on, I had more energy, engagement, passion, hunger, and an aura of happiness, than I could ever remember. I had found purposeful engagement and was connecting it with my value within the work I was doing, and a thousand wild horses couldn't hold me back.

In my reflections of the changes that I wanted to make in my life to reverse the unhappiness that I was experiencing, I had realised something. That deep down, I wanted to be empowered to make an impact on people, influence and inspire them to make positive changes, and enrich their lives. It was only when I took the time to self-reflect and explore who I was and what I truly wanted, that I realised this: it's funny what a decluttered mind can do.

More importantly, what I had managed to do was connect this with my value, in leveraging and leaning into what I felt were my superpowers, in communication and storytelling. From there, I converted it into my work, in writing my first book, and unbeknown to me then, my future books and wider speaking and consulting engagements.

What I had done was identified what purposeful engagement meant for me, connected it to the value I can offer and manifested it through the work I wanted to do.

I had now made the switch. Who I am and the value I offer now defines what I do.

Reflection moment

What aspects of your work align with your values? If there are gaps, how might you go about closing them?

If you remember, I had left it late in the changes I was making, I hadn't turned the page to a new chapter in time, so my adjustments, arguably are quite extreme. However, it is easy to forget the importance of aligning your purpose with the work that you do. I enjoyed exploring this topic, with some very experienced and successful people in their fields.

Dion Smith – Global Leader | Board Member | Speaker

Rediscovering career happiness begins with reconnecting to your "why." It's easy to get lost in the hustle and routine, but realigning with what truly drives you is the foundation of career fulfilment. Start by asking yourself what initially sparked your passion. Was it solving complex problems, leading teams, or creating innovative solutions? Then, consider if your current role still ignites that same fire. If not, perhaps it's time for a shift, whether it's changing roles, industries, or simply redefining your goals in your current environment. The key is to pause, reflect, and make deliberate choices to move towards what excites and energises you.

Andrew MacAskill – LinkedIn Top Voice: Careers | Author

Happiness, not just career happiness, is about aligning who you are with what you do. Your identity is not your job, so it is about de-coupling yourself from this and giving yourself the permission to explore. When looking at your work and role specifically, I feel it needs to align to three elements. Firstly, your head. Does it give you the growth and stimulation you need? Secondly your heart. Does it allow you to bring your full self to work each day, aligning with your purpose and values? This is so important, and I have seen more people burnout due to lack of values alignment rather than long hours. Thirdly, your wallet. You need to feel like you are getting paid fairly for the value you are creating and that it works for the life you live outside of work. When you are aligned, you don't have those Sunday dreads, you start each day with energy, clarity, knowing what you want to achieve. I know people who whilst having sold their businesses for millions, are extremely unhappy because they no longer aligned in who they are and what they do. If you do find yourself getting lost in this, a great way to rediscover your purpose, engagement and value, is to mentor people. It is a great way to remind them, and yourself, of who you are and the value that you have.

Simon Moyle – CEO | Non-Exec | Mentor | Investor

If people are re-evaluating themselves, looking for change, then the first thing to do is to believe in themselves. After twenty years at Dixons, I had lost my enjoyment, my spark for the role and the business. I had an experience where I asked to leave, I took a risk, as I didn't have a degree, I only ever knew *Dixons*, and so I had to believe in myself to do this. In the end, I got the call from the founder of *Vivup* and an opportunity to run the business for them. So that's why believing in yourself, keeping the faith is incredibly important.

Investing in yourself

"Where do I start?" This was a question that I hadn't asked myself for quite some time. When you spend 20 years in a field of work, I would suggest that you could call yourself an expert, or an experienced pair of hands at what you do. While I had lost my confidence and engagement in what I was doing, I still had plenty of achievements, and learnings, so technically, I could be called an expert. However, in deciding to start something new, explore a new purposeful path, I faced that very real question of, "Where do I start?" because now I was at the start of the cycle again, or was I?

In my mind, in pursuing a self-employed path spanning that of an author, speaker and coach, I was now entering into an arena which I hadn't played in before, and in reaction to this, I probably did what many would do: make a list. I listed out all the areas that I needed to learn and develop, which in turn would give me the invested skills so that I could perform the value creation that I wanted to do. However, this wasn't completely true. In my panic over re-skilling, fuelled by a fear of the unknown and a sprinkle of imposter syndrome, I had overlooked the skills I had developed over the past twenty or more years.

When challenging myself on this, I realised that much of what I felt I needed to invest in, such as project management, writing, editing, marketing, branding, competitor research, building new connections, distribution, public speaking, social media, digital content creation, I had in fact, been investing in this through my educational years and in every day of my working life. I have always been investing in myself, I just hadn't recognised it, until now. So, when it came to the question therefore of, "Where do I start?" I found that the on-ramp was not as steep as originally anticipated.

What I have learnt is that if you treat today as a learning opportunity in everything that you do, then you are continually investing in yourself, and what this does is prepare you for when tomorrow comes. While I recognise this now, in the past I had viewed investing in myself through the lens of it being functional for the job role that I did. So, in a very strange way, it was more about developing my performance at my functional job, as opposed to developing my performance as Jamie, the human being.

By thinking about how you can continually invest in yourself and putting it into practice, you are developing the value that you offer. When you then connect this with purposeful engagement, you can accelerate and amplify the benefit. Whether you are in a working role and happy, thinking about changing, or even in the change, investing in you not only helps, but can also be the difference between making it happen or not.

Reflection moment

How seriously do you take investing in yourself? List out some of the areas which you could invest time in that would increase the value you bring.

I discussed "investing in yourself" with Hanna Larsson, Founder of *Huntrs* and LinkedIn Top Voice. Hanna is an advocate for helping people to create their own value, pursue purposeful engagement and explore entrepreneurship and working flexibility. Having done this herself, Hanna cites the investment in you as a cornerstone of making it happen. Hanna says, "If people want to start to build their own value, outside of their current role, then they start by learning how to monetise their knowledge and build an audience. From here, they then start to identify the skills they need to level up, actively build their personal brand, and to treat themselves like a product, so they can start to get some additional income streams in." I was also interested to get Hanna's take on how people strike a balance of pursuing this while in their current role, "The key is not to leave their existing job too soon. It is important that you get started and then build it step by step. When you have a reliable income stream, and you can see that it has the potential to get bigger, this may well be the time where you now dedicate yourself fully to it and leave your existing job."

Whilst this might not be for everyone, Hanna's approach highlights the importance of placing the value, and investing in that, in the person first and foremost. I was also keen to get further reflections from our other experts, and their specific thoughts on how people could go about investing in themselves.

Dion Smith – Global Leader | Board Member | Speaker

Investing in yourself is one of the most rewarding things you can do, and it all starts with a mindset shift, recognising that growth is not optional, it's essential. Whether it's through formal education, gaining certifications, or developing soft skills like emotional intelligence, investing in yourself means committing to becoming a better version of you. But change doesn't happen overnight. It's about taking small, consistent steps toward your goals. Seek mentors who challenge you, surround yourself with people who inspire you, and never be afraid to pivot when something no longer serves you. Personal growth is the fuel that powers career satisfaction and long-term success.

Andrew MacAskill – LinkedIn Top Voice: Careers | Author

Vision drives decision, so firstly you need to ideally be clear on what you are trying to achieve. Once you have that, then you need to become the CEO of your career and ask yourself, what are the skills I need, who are the connections I should build, what personal brand do I need to have, adjust my CV, LinkedIn profile, is my narrative and story aligned. Then you need to make it happen and invest in yourself. Being self-aware of your strengths and weaknesses is also important, yes, your weaknesses need to be at a base level, but it is your strengths and your superpowers which make the difference and leaning into those will be a greater investment for you.

Niraj Kapur - LinkedIn Top Voice | Managing Director

Investing in your mindset will make all the difference. So how do you do this? The easiest thing you can do is to get a journal and spend 5 minutes a night writing down your thoughts on what you are grateful for, and any mistakes you might have made. In the morning, ensure you have a vision board in place, which identifies your goals and dreams, and just look. These two activities will help to shift your perspective and mindset to a positive outlook, and by doing this, you will achieve more in life. This, for me, is one of the greatest investments you can do for yourself.

Simon Moyle - CEO | Non-Exec | Mentor | Investor

Having a network of people and not burning bridges is a very important thing and by taking the time to build this network, you are investing in yourself. This isn't about having a formal professional network, but it is about having people who you can talk to, share with, to get guidance, advice and support from. I would not have been able to achieve what I have done, if I didn't have people who I could contact, engage with, learn from, employ, and work with.

With a mindset of seeing you, first and foremost, as the value in what you can create, makes it easier for you to continuously invest in yourself. Through skill development, learning experiences, building connections, and exploring new opportunities, the outcome is to help you become the best version of yourself and put you in a position to apply your value in ways that positively contribute to your long-lasting happiness.

Balance

Whether this is down to me or whether this is down to the working machine, I am not completely sure, but what I am sure about is this. From the moment I took my first job, through to my last job, as my roles and responsibilities got bigger and bigger and my pay grade got higher and higher, so did the coverage of the working percentage in my life. The way it has felt that if you take more, you must give more, so, you can have the promotion and the pay rise, but this means we become more present in your life and need more time off you.

This has been my trajectory, and a trajectory which led me to an unhealthy balance at this stage of my life. Work took over, I became unhappy at work, and given the coverage it had in my life, this meant the wider impacts were being felt. As I mentioned, maybe this was down to me, in that I was not only relentlessly pursuing bigger roles, but also because I failed to set and reset the boundaries which protected me from work entering non-work time. I used to see balance as a constant tug-of-war between work and life, a fight to keep the scales even. But looking back, I see it's more about integration and blend. Real balance isn't about dividing time between competing parts but about making space for all of life to coexist.

I think of time and energy as the two most precious resources we have, limited yet powerful. Balance for me, is making the choices of where we spend them consciously rather than being pulled in directions that don't serve us. If we can get ourselves into a position whereby we are in control of where we are intentionally spending our time and energy, then we can define our balance.

Is there a perfect balance? There's no 'perfect' when it comes to balance; it's a moving target, a flexible state that changes with life's demands, and so striving for a perfect ideal can and will create unrealistic expectations and in turn frustrations. The key is accepting that balance is a flexible, ongoing process, and not a fixed and perfect point.

Today my approach to balance has changed, but then so have my priorities. I wanted to get back in control of time and energy, establish personal boundaries, and decide where I would use the best of it to create value through my work. I took a drastic step to reset this, exceptional you could say, in stepping away from an established full time and pay-rolled career and choosing to become self-employed, pursuing new dreams. But it wasn't just about this, it was also about balancing my time and energy across the other areas of importance to me, our other four branches, all of which are focussed on prioritising my long-lasting happiness.

I made a change in my life to reset the balance. Am I financially better off for it? For now, no. Am I happier and have a greater control of balance in my life for it? Yes, and at this stage of my life, this is more valuable to me. We will all be at different stages in our lives and what comes with that are different priorities. Having a focus on your balance, checking yourself on this, and being proactively in control of it enables you to strike a healthy and relevant use of your time and energy to create the value you need.

Resetting my balance took a major life change, but it doesn't always have to be drastic. Small adjustments can create powerful shifts too, it might mean committing to finish work at a certain hour, even taking a break. What matters is simply starting. Whether it's a big leap or a small step, any effort to reclaim our balance is a step in taking back control of our happiness.

I was interested to get a take on this topic of balance and its connection with the workplace with Ryan Hopkins, bestselling author, TedX speaker, LinkedIn Top Voice on wellbeing, and Chief Impact Officer at JAAQ. Ryan says, "It's not an organisations responsibility to improve your long-lasting happiness, however it is their responsibility not to worsen it. The question for organisations is how we can create the environment where you can focus on being your best self. It is about giving you the tools you need and respect how you spend your time whether that be work or other things which provide you that balance. By respecting how people use their time and energy, will allow them to really engage with their purpose both inside and outside of work. Providing that safety, flexibility and autonomy in the workplace, where you can balance the output of work with the other things they might want to do, will positively contribute towards happiness, engagement and wellbeing. Organisations need to realise that there is no performance long-term without wellbeing."

Balance for happiness, was also a driving force behind the changes which Hasan Kubba, speaker, coach and bestselling author of *The Unfair Advantage,* made in his career. Hasan said, "I had to become the designer of my professional life and to take that proactive approach in controlling my own destiny. I could not find the right balance for me when being told what to do, or having restrictive boundaries placed around me by a boss, a company or an employee handbook. It took me a couple of years to find the courage to make the leap, but when I did, feeling this sense of freedom and balance was big for me and for my long-lasting happiness. Don't get me wrong, there are always difficult days, however I remind myself that I chose this, I am in control, have balance, and this gives me the motivation and energy to push on."

Reflection moment

Do you have a healthy balance? Draw a pie chart and split out within it your balance; include the time you spend on creating value through work, time on the other branches, and don't forget time for when you sleep. Once done ask yourself, is this the right balance for you?

Reflecting on this branch which is centred on creating value, its coverage and importance in life, my own experiences, and the insights of others, in many respects, I wish that I had exposure to this when I was starting out in my career. If you are a young adult reading this book, then you might be familiar with Jack Parsons, LinkedIn Top Voice and co-founder and Group CEO at Youth Group. Given Jack's dedication to supporting over 100 million youths with, amongst other areas, their work goals in particular, I wanted to get his reflections on this topic of value and happiness for those starting out in their careers.

Value and happiness interview with Jack Parsons

What does happiness mean to Jack?

Happiness has become more than just an aspiration; it's something I work towards every day, shaping my choices, actions, and the energy I bring into the world. For me, happiness is found in alignment, being true to who I am and fostering connections with others that bring purpose and meaning.

How can working value connect with happiness?

Happiness in this arena, is about finding alignment between your work and values. When you get there, sustain it by setting meaningful goals and creating space for growth. Happiness is a habit, it's cultivated through commitment, not just circumstance.

How do you start and move forward?

Start with self-reflection. Ask yourself what genuinely brings you joy and where you find meaning. It's okay to start small; even small steps toward purpose can spark big changes. From there, invest in yourself, which means focusing on skills that excite and challenge you. Building resilience, adaptability, and emotional intelligence are key. These qualities help us grow and handle whatever life throws our way.

How do you persevere through the challenges?

When the journey feels long, remind yourself why you started. Surround yourself with people who lift you up and celebrate your progress, no matter how small. Persistence and self-compassion are essential, especially when setbacks arise.

What advice would you give to yourself when starting out?

I'd tell young Jack, "Be kind to yourself and embrace the journey. Believe in your potential and stay true to your values, even when the road gets tough. The setbacks will be worth it."

In Jack's reflections, what strikes me are the consistencies of advice that we have already explored in this fifth and final branch, value. The key message here is that whatever stage you are at in your life, working journey or career, it is incredibly important to continuously keep yourself in check. Given the amount of time you invest in this area of your life, its longevity and impact on your long-lasting happiness is profound, so whatever stage you are at, always remember the importance of your value.

Key reflection

Our fifth and final branch, value, represents a significant part of our life. What we do will help us create income which in turn enables us to live. However, given its coverage, there is a heightened importance on ensuring that the process of value creation contributes positively towards our long-lasting happiness, and not the other way around.

Takeaways

- Your job doesn't define you. It is important to remind yourself that it is you as a person and your skills which creates the real value, and not the job itself.

- Finding and connecting your purpose with how you create value will unlock a level of engagement and happiness in you which at times can be quite magical.

- A mindset of continually investing in yourself will both enable and make it easier for you to explore and take opportunities to create value.

- Creating value to gain income to live, takes up a lot of our time. Therefore, it is important to ensure that you are in control of how you balance this within the context of your life, and the other four branches.

Sprouting happiness reflections

Reflecting on this branch, challenge yourself on how you are aligning purposeful engagement, investing in yourself and balance, not just create value, but also positively impact your long-lasting happiness?

"MEASURE WHAT YOU TREASURE"

Part 4:

Never Give Up

I kept turning around and looking back, not wanting to fully let go of the habits, routines, behaviours which had become ingrained into my day-to-day life. Whilst I knew they no longer served me, in fact I knew they were damaging me, I was still being drawn back to the comfort and familiarity they provided. Were the changes that I needed to make for the sake of my long-lasting happiness, just too hard to make?

When faced with the prospect of change, no matter how big or how small, it is hard, and as humans the prospect of change can be very daunting. This stems from many different elements across our physical, social, psychological and neurological needs, and over the last sixteen months it has felt that all of them have been doing their very best to pull me back. Over the last five chapters we have explored through our five branches to living a happy and balanced life, what to focus on, what can be done, and how to make it happen. However, and more broadly, when it comes to change, we will face obstacles, we will wobble and at times, we will want to give up, and I know this, because it has plagued my mind every single day. I haven't given up because each passing day becomes a little easier, raises the baseline of my long-lasting happiness, and reduces how often I look back over my shoulder.

So, having made the decision to prioritise your long-lasting happiness, with the five branches now firmly at the forefront of your change, what else is important to consider so that we never give up?

Remember your "why"

The changes which I have implemented in my life, span all five branches, and all of which have required reflection, decision and action. Looking back, it has been a lot, and at times maybe too much for me to manage. In these moments, I reminded myself of the one thing which was fuelling my appetite for change, my "why". This is your driving force, your purpose, what motivates you to embrace change, stay resilient, and prioritise long-lasting happiness. Take yourself back to the story branch. Here I highlighted the importance of establishing your narrative and living the story that you want to live. Having this at the forefront of your mind will help to immerse you in the reasons as to why you are prioritising your long-lasting happiness.

I have my narrative saved as a note on my phone, accessible for when I need it, written as a commitment and reminder to myself as to why my long-lasting happiness is important to me. I check it, not every day, but at times when I feel myself doubting, wobbling a little, questioning what tomorrow might bring. That important reminder of my "why", my purpose, keeps me in check and calibrated to my path. There are many techniques that you can use to regain clarity and focus of your "why", here are a few to think about:

1. **Visualise it**: Create a vision board with associated reminders or design a digital reminder and apply it to your desktop or phone wallpaper.

2. **Write it**: Could be on your phone, post-it notes, within a journal, or even printed out physically.

3. **Set reminders**: Use your phone's diary and set messages centred on your "why" in advance to pop up at key times.

4. **Share your "why"**: By telling others, they can be there to remind you of your "why" at moments of need. My brother is brilliant at this.

5. **Association**: Be sure to link what you are doing with your "why", it acts as a reminder that your decisions and actions are fully aligned.

Whilst tools can help you reconnect with your "why" and purpose, sometimes hearing how others have navigated this, especially in difficult times, can provide important perspective. Ryan Hopkins shared with me how he used this during certain periods in his life. "There is a book that changed my life called *Man's Search for Meaning* which is about a holocaust survivor who explores the notion that the concept of happiness is about having a purpose and living aligned to a purpose, and this was what kept him alive. Personally, I have struggled a long time with my mental health, and I used to have to develop these crazy goals like walk across Spain on my own and push through blisters and pain, but I asked myself why do I need to do this? So, learning to find purpose for me through others and giving as opposed to pushing myself into horrible situations, has been a journey of discovery for me."

"Throughout my life, the big moments of learning have come from moments of unhappiness. I remember breaking my leg and my ankle which in turn stripped away my job as a sparky and playing rugby, two things which were part of my identity. There have been multiple things like that, such as addiction, an eating disorder, suicidal thoughts, which have all led to me focussing on the wrong things and looking for validation from others, rather than understanding who I am. I have been in a lot of pain and difficulty over the years, but it now improves because of the increased understanding of myself, and the alignment I have to my purpose, in sharing my stories to help people not end up where I did. This gives me that energy, passion, and authenticity to keep going and to change the world. There are times when the clarity of your purpose may become hazy, and this can make things harder, create setbacks, but the key is to get clarity back and regain that laser focus on your purpose, because if it is strong enough, then you will never give up."

Your "why", crafted well, and regularly reinforced, will act as both encouragement and assurance not just through periods of change, but also through, well, everyday life. I dip and I worry, but when I do I return to my "why", make sure that you do too.

Confronting fear

I sat there, hand on the mouse, finger hovering and readying itself to click the button which said, "Publish". Having spent twenty years in full-time employment, working in senior roles in major global brands, always having a predictable salary each month, being at the top of my game, technically capable, and extremely experienced, this moment represented more than you could imagine. I was about to not just release a book, something that I have never done before, but also announce publicly that I was self-employed and not continuing along my previous path. To say that I was confronting fear would be an understatement.

First, my mind was flooded with anxiety, worrying about the potential negative scenarios that would present themselves. What if the book quality was seen as poor, it received terrible reviews, people considered me unemployable, what if all my hard work for the last 20 years just collapses in on itself? This was then followed by self-doubt; I am not an author, I am an imposter, I can't be self-employed, I can't competently work primarily on my own, I can't generate the income

I need to survive. Then came failure. "It won't work, Jamie, the book will be a flop, you will never create the income you need to survive, you will fail yourself and your family. Finally, self-sabotage kicked in and took control, instead of hitting publish, my mind and body moved the mouse slightly to the left and instead hit the save button. What should have been a moment of achievement and new beginnings, became a moment vandalised by fear.

Fear had won; however, its victory was short-lived. Minutes later, after sharing with my wife how I felt about the fear that I was confronting (not for the first time, I might add) I was back in my chair. I grabbed the mouse, moved the pointer, and with a smile on my face, and wife by my side, I said, "I'll never give up" and hit publish.

Over the last sixteen months I have been confronting fear every day, I am both aware of it and of how it can impact me. However, what I will say is that the intensity and strength of it has been reducing, why? Firstly, I am no longer afraid to confront fear. I know that it is part of life, part of my journey in prioritising long-lasting happiness, and that it is going to happen, so I see it more as a challenge rather than a deterrent. But secondly, I always try to evidence it. Much of my fears come from within, self-inflicted, manifesting through my own thoughts. So, my way to counter them is to try to evidence it, bring some objectivity and rationalisation to it, and do you know the result? 99% of the time I can't. It's like fearing a debt which doesn't need paying.

No fear is worth more than your long-lasting happiness. So, when you face it, remember this; recognise it for what it is, challenge it with evidence, and confront it with the right tools, support and mindset. It's worth the effort because on the other side of fear, lies freedom, growth and what you are working toward.

Reflection moment

Are your fears preventing you from prioritising your long-lasting happiness? Note down a fear that gets in your way and;

- Name it
- Challenge it with evidence
- List what you need to confront it

Perfectionism

When I began this journey, I came from a place of deep unhappiness in many of the five branches. For some, I was starting out afresh, others were more about re-aligning to this new chapter in my story. I found this both daunting and dangerous because of my perfectionism. Not ideal in some respects, especially when you are trying to set new pathways and trying to get started with the change.

I found this particularly challenging because I was pushing myself into new territories within the branches such as story, value, physical, and inner self. This sense of newness and uncertainty was triggering a desire for perfectionism, a safety blanket of sorts, in ensuring that what I was going to do and where I was heading, was perfectly mapped out. However, this was paralysing, and perfectionism can trap you. I would catch myself overthinking plans, researching endlessly, and delaying action because things didn't feel perfectly mapped out. It was exhausting, counterproductive and eventually, I had to accept that imperfection and simply starting were far more important than perfect execution.

Comparison was another hurdle I had to confront. As Theodore Roosevelt famously said, "Comparison is the thief of joy." Social media makes this especially challenging, giving us a constant shop window into other people's lives. It's so easy to scroll through and think, why am I not further along? Why don't I look like that? Why haven't I achieved that yet? But comparison is a false metric. Every person is on a different path, with unique challenges and strengths, no one is the same.

I am not innocent in this, I would look at what other people were doing especially in the branches of value, physical and inner self, trying to get a gauge on where I should be and when. But all it ever did was leave me frustrated and disheartened. Like with perfectionism, I've learned to recognise when I'm falling into the comparison trap and actively pull myself back.

Perfectionism and comparison combined make for a potent cocktail of "give up juice", that can cloud perspective and derail your progress. They can interfere with your expectations, pushing you to unrealistic levels and false perceptions of where you are vs where you think you should be. That's why it is so important that you stay grounded in your daily life and be self-aware of when that perfectionism and comparison cocktail might tempt you for a sip.

Time

Let's consider one of the most challenging physical feats in the world: climbing Mount Everest. How long do you think it takes? The answer: around sixty-six days. It's an important reminder that achieving something monumental takes time, commitment, and pacing. When embarking on my journey sixteen months ago, while not quite Everest, I knew that I would need to give myself time.

I didn't start everything across the five branches in one go; I knew that I had to pace them at different times, allowing myself to create and settle into new habits and routines, before introducing new ones.

Here's how it unfolded for me:

1. **Month 1**: Establishing my story had to come first, giving me purpose, direction and a narrative I could align the other four branches to.
2. **Month 2**: Next came the value branch. This was crucial because it was a major source of my unhappiness. I began writing my book, connecting with new people and investing in the tools and knowledge to support my journey.
3. **Month 3**: With more clarity, momentum, and settled into the change, I shifted focus to the people branch. Whilst already

in a good place, I wanted to re-assess. Who did I want to spend more time with? Who was draining my energy?

4. **Month 6**: Even with the book launched, and some progress in the value branch, the challenges of change were present, and things were feeling slightly chaotic. It felt natural that this would be a good time to look inward and focus on the inner self branch.

5. **Month 9**: Finally, with routines and habits firmly established, a more predictable weekly schedule, and a newly sparked motivation, I now turned to the physical branch. I knew this would require commitment and discipline, given the level of change I needed to make, and this was the right time to start.

Looking back, I didn't plan it this way, it just evolved naturally. I was very mindful that while I wanted to achieve everything, including a significant improvement in my long-lasting happiness, all at once and almost instantly, this wasn't realistic. If I hadn't allowed myself the time to make changes, find consistency, form routines and habits, embed discipline, it would have had the opposite effect.

Whatever level of change and focus you are striving for in sprouting your long-lasting happiness, be sure to give yourself the time you need. Life is busy, and time is often in short supply, so be realistic with your pacing, expectations and where you place priority.

Time can either be your greatest ally or your greatest excuse. Choose it and use it wisely.

Track, reflect, propel

Life doesn't stand still, and neither do our five branches to a happy and balanced life. With each day we make decisions, act, react, and exert energy, all of which create ripples in our lives. These seemingly small steps, the one percenters, shape our growth and long-lasting happiness. By recognising the path you've walked, embracing both the good and the bad, and celebrating progress, you can use it to pave the way forward, and keep you connected to the long-lasting happiness you desire. Here are 3 important steps which have kept me aligned and committed:

1. **Track**: Measure what you treasure. Whatever you value within each of the five branches, identify and track it. Remember, this will be unique to you, only you truly understand what drives your baseline of long-lasting happiness. Tracking progress isn't about perfection, it is about intention and consistency.

2. **Reflect**: Take a moment to pause and reflect. This isn't just the measurements, it is about the feelings, emotions, and experiences along the way. These reflections offer you profound insights into yourself, helping you grow and learn along the way.

3. **Propel**: Let this rich everyday knowledge inform your tomorrow. It is a propellant that can inspire fresh choices, decisions and actions that positively impact your long-lasting happiness.

Journaling is a powerful way to engage with this process. Whether through writing, audio, or another medium, it will help you to digest and celebrate all the incredible progress you are making, the learnings, and will help to stay in touch with your sprouting happiness lifestyle. For extra support, check out the *Sprouting Happiness Journal* (available on Amazon), specially designed to help you track, reflect and propel your journey of long-lasting happiness.

Reflection moment

Do you capture your reflections? Take a moment to identify one key learning from your day and ask yourself: How can I use this insight to take an action that will positively impact my long-lasting happiness?

Focus on the benefits

By my own admission I am a positive and optimistic person. Whilst this can catch me out sometimes, especially when setting expectations on myself, I find that it helps me to focus on the benefits of what it is I am doing. You will hear me say, "eyes on the prize", an affirmation I share with myself especially when things aren't quite going how I envisaged or at the pace I would like. It acts as a magnet, pulling me forward and keeping me focused.

We've already talked about the importance of remembering your "why", but it's equally important to remember the benefits that will come with it too. By focussing on the five branches, each will bring incredible and unique rewards to your life. I know, because they are happening to me. Think about how each branch can bring benefit to your life:

- ◆ The **Story** branch shapes the way you view yourself and how you want to interact with the world around you – keeping your decisions and actions aligned who you are.

- ◆ The **People** branch, whether inside or outside the workplace, enables you to nurture relationships and keep you connected with and surrounded by those who will positively impact your happiness.

- ◆ The **Physical** branch gives your body and mind the energy to fully engage every day and will enable you to do things that you want to do.

- ◆ The **Inner Self** branch keeps that inner flame burning bright and tall. Nurturing and being kind to your inner self will positively influence how you feel, behave and act.

- ◆ The **Value** branch focuses on the engagement and contribution of you first and foremost. Through this you will create more value from the most important asset you own, you.

These benefits merely scratch the surface of what's possible when you focus on your long-lasting happiness. Imagine yourself taking action and experiencing these rewards, how would that feel? When you focus on the benefits, keep them front and centre, they will pull you along when you need it, and whilst they might not come immediately, come they will.

Any form of change is hard. Committing to it and following it through is not easy, however the challenges you face of doing it will always outweigh the challenges of not doing it at all. When doubts creep in remember your "why". Find the courage to confront your fears, let go of perfectionism, give yourself time, track your progress, reflect on it, use what you have learned from it to propel yourself forward, and focus on the benefits, they will pull you through.

It's ok to pause, adjust your path, or try something new. But as my Dad always said,

"Never give up."

Key reflection

Focusing on long-lasting happiness will require change, and the challenge of this is very real. Putting ourselves in the best position get started with our five branches, making them happen, and never giving up will enable us to push through and enjoy the benefits that a happy and balanced life will bring.

Takeaways

♦ Remembering your "why" will keep you connected to your driving force for change and need for long-lasting happiness.

♦ Fears are a given. Finding the courage to identify, evidence and confront them, will allow you to enjoy what is on the other side.

♦ Give yourself time. The level of change you want to make will impact the time that you need. Make sure you have enough of it to build consistency, habits and routines.

♦ Measure what you treasure, track your progress, reflect and use the learnings to propel you forward.

♦ Never forget the benefits of positively impacting your long-lasting happiness, you will find them in all five branches. They will pull you forward when you need it the most.

Sprouting happiness reflections

How likely are you to give up? Prioritising your long-lasting will require change, looking back on this chapter, which considerations resonate with you the most? How can you implement them into your life?

"A PICTURE CAN PAINT
A THOUSAND WORDS,
A STORY
CAN CHANGE A
THOUSAND LIVES"

Part 5:

Stories. Change. Lives.

If you have read my first book, you'll know how deeply I value the power of storytelling. Stories are the thread which tie us all together, helping us to learn, connect, grow, share and heal. They can help light up paths of new perspective, act as sparks of motivation and change, or create magical moments of pure inspiration. Simply put: Stories. Change. Lives.

Throughout this book, you've read about my journey and how I've approached prioritising and sprouting my long-lasting happiness. Now it's time to hear from others. This chapter offers a collection of relatable, real-life reflections from twenty-nine incredible people. It is a beautiful collection of authenticity, honesty and vulnerability, from the hearts of those who have supported me during my journey of change. Each perspective is unique, highlighting there is no single right path to happiness. Instead, they remind us that prioritising long-lasting happiness is always worthwhile.

Take your time, savour their reflections and let them inspire your own journey.

Gavin Mackenzie: Founder – *Nest Property* | Developer

Perception: Happiness is about being fulfilled daily. For me, a moment of happiness isn't true happiness, as if there is a cloud that sits above it, you can quite quickly go back to an unhappier place. Happiness exists when there are no highs, and you still feel content.

Impacts on happiness: Having the freedom to spend my time how I want to, gives me a great sense of happiness. On the flip side, what will bring me unhappiness is being restricted, told what to do, or if someone else is trying to negatively influence my decisions for their own gain.

Focussing on happiness: I proactively work on identifying what makes me unhappy, and then I change it. For example, I believe there is a very fine line between your professional and personal life. Some people see them as two separate things, but if you're unhappy at work, you'll be unhappy at home, and vice versa, so change it. I also make time for myself and what makes me happy. When I'm in a happier state, I can give so much more to other people and build better relationships.

Stories that I tell myself: I remind myself that life is very short, that I shouldn't take it too seriously and to focus on what makes me happy. I also believe it is important to have a routine that works for you, and tweak it if things aren't working. By constantly reflecting and adjusting, you'll have a happier mindset and lifestyle.

When living a happy life: I can achieve anything and everything!

Sabrina Oostburg: TN 2022 Olympic Weightlifting Champion

Perception: For me, I view happiness as a combination of day-to-day things which stack; they gain momentum and this results in joy, leading to contentment in your life.

Focussing on happiness: I am very proactive in doing things which activate my five senses, because this is a big driver of happiness for me. So, engaging in the sports I love, working out, listening to music, getting out into nature, watching the sunset, even eating my favourite burger, I never take these things for granted and embrace all of them. I am also aware of what pulls on my happiness and one area is neglecting myself. The reason being is that I always want to be in a fit state to be available and to help people.

Stories that I tell myself: When I was in middle school, I got hit with a big injury - breaking my leg. This had a huge impact on me as I had to work for almost a year to recover and during that time I felt that I had lost my identity. What helped me, and still inspires me today, was the mindset I chose to have. I could have opted for a negative mindset, "poor me", but instead I went for the positive mindset of coming back stronger, and sure enough, I did.

Imogen Davis: Heptathlete | Olympic Prospect

Perception: For me it is a whole host of feelings including contentment, success, pride, confidence, being at peace and being present in the moment. In many respects, it is about having a deep understanding and unconditional acceptance of yourself.

Impacts on happiness: A big promoter of happiness for me is knowing that I have given 100% in everything that I do so that I can reach my full potential. Other drivers include my sport, being with friends, having a support network, and spending time with family. If I feel that I am failing or wanting to quit, letting people down, or being injured, then this is my warning light that something is wrong and I'm unhappy or stressed.

Focussing on happiness: The work I am doing now with my sports psychologist in understanding and re-wiring my mindset, is making a huge difference to me. Creating the right environment, both physically and mentally, for myself to be successful as an athlete is a core focus for me.

Stories that I tell myself: The only story I hear every day, is that niggling feeling that I must conquer it, whatever "it" may be. This is because the feeling of quitting is much worse.

When living a happy life: Being in a state of long-lasting happiness, allows you to mentally give 100% in everything that you do. It sets me up to achieve everything that I want to achieve.

Nikky Ricks: Fitness Professional | IFBB Pro Bodybuilder

Perception: For me, happiness comes from within yourself as a person. It's about accepting who you are and being comfortable in your own skin, but also wanting to push your boundaries. I feel that being happy is a choice you make when you wake up every morning.

Impacts on happiness: People can impact my happiness both ways. My core friends are the ones who constantly pull my happiness up, always there for me when I need them. On the other hand, people who are selfish, negative, and untruthful, they will drag my happiness down. Exercise and training help to lift my happiness, plus they also act as a great mental relief for me.

Focussing on happiness: My grandfather told me something which has stuck with me all my life, "a tidy room is a tidy mind". So, I always get up, make my bed, and ensure that the place is tidy. This sets me up for the day. The other thing I always do is not to let things fester. If I can action something then I will do it. For me there is no point in letting it play on my mind.

Stories that I tell myself: There is one saying that always plays over in my mind, "Is it me?". Everything we experience in life is based on our actions and reactions, and so I am always checking myself, asking that question, "Is it me?".

Harry Beech: Lifestyle Personal Trainer

Perception: For me, happiness is about being comfortable with and loving yourself fully. This isn't a static scale or measure, and I believe you must continually work on it and grow it, but you are doing this from a solid baseline.

Impacts on happiness: The gym is a big driver of my happiness; in fact, it has saved me in so many ways, in this environment I really feel at home. Also, the work I do with my charity and as a personal trainer, allows me to help others, which I find extremely rewarding. The only major pull on my happiness I can note is if someone was to question my integrity or my values, I wouldn't be comfortable with this.

Focussing on happiness: I love doing new things, learning, exploring places I haven't been before. These all allow me to grow and share that knowledge with others in the hope of helping them. Spending quality time with my girlfriend is also incredibly important to me.

Stories that I tell myself: I spent a lot of my childhood not knowing who I was, and this led me to feeling lost. When my son passed away, this was a significant moment in my life as wherever he is, I want to make him proud. This drive is with me every day, and it plays a role in both the actions I take and the help I provide.

Niraj Kapur: LinkedIn Top Voice | Managing Director

Perception: Happiness is what you decide and not what society tells you. For me, it is centred around three things; giving, supporting, being charitable and gratitude, and I ensure these occur daily.

Impacts on happiness: What makes me unhappy are people who make excuses in life but do nothing about it. They might complain about very real problems and issues, however when pushed on addressing them, they have no intention to address them and they compare yourself to others. This for me is a downward spiral of unhappiness.

Focussing on happiness: People don't decide their futures, they decide their habits, and their habits decide their futures. So, I have habits I do every day. I write in my gratitude journal, I walk in nature, do my 10k steps, I enjoy my flat white, I take a cold shower, I take regular breaks, I network with people. I choose the habits which make me happy and allow me to live the life that I want.

Stories that I tell myself: I have a vision board; this drives me every day and it is centred on serving other people.

When living a happy life: I wake up feeling grateful for everything I have and thinking about what three people I am going to help, whether it be my partner, my parents, my daughter, my step kids, those who I coach and my wider network.

Ryan Hopkins: Author | Speaker | Wellbeing Expert

Perception: I feel that definitions here are important. I see short term happiness as a fleeting emotion much like anger or sadness, however I see long term happiness, or joy, as much deeper, centred around finding and being aligned to your purpose, meaning, and for me this sustainable long-lasting happiness is what it should be about.

Impacts on happiness: Detractors for me would be not being able to work in the way that I want to work, stagnation, and going backwards. In fact, its anything that prevents me from living my purpose and my alignment.

Focussing on happiness: Fitness plays a huge part in my long-lasting happiness, balance and mental health. It is the only time when I don't have to think, I can switch off, I am calm, and so moving is something of high importance that I need to do.

Stories that I tell myself: I want to be this cheeky geezer who can speak with insight, data, credibility and challenge the status quo. This does help my self-belief, and I know that I am only just getting started here.

When living a happy life: Working to leave a legacy in society on the importance of wellbeing. That will be through leading change in legislation, the way healthcare is delivered, transforming the workplace, this is what I want to be remembered for.

Simon Moyle: CEO | Non-Exec | Mentor | Investor

Perception: For me the journey, and the people with me, is where happiness comes from, and not the result. Being able to provide for the kids, create experiences and memories we could share, support them through university, and being able to give them the life that my parents worked hard for, but couldn't quite get for us. Also bringing happiness to others, in work and in friendship groups, this is what gives me happiness.

Impacts on happiness: Flexibility to then be able to give back and to be there for people gives me a lot of happiness. Unfairness is a big driver of unhappiness for me, I don't like seeing this and the impact it has on people, and people who ask for so much as opposed respecting to be offered first. For this reason, I have always treated people fairly, with respect and offered when ready, and in turn have seen the positive impact that it can have.

Focussing on happiness: I am a very focussed and target-driven person, and I like to incorporate this - gamify it even - into my life. Whether it be setting a target for time away with my wife or buying tickets to the football. I used this to drive me to do the things which give me happiness, as sometimes it's easy to get complacent, not do it, or even forget.

Stories that I tell myself: There isn't any overarching story for me, it is more centred on being happy with the contribution I have made and the impact that I have had on other people. There is nothing more satisfying than seeing a group of people, together, having fun and knowing that I have played a part in creating that moment.

When living a happy life: For me it truly is about giving back to other people. I am in a position now where I can do this both through time, knowledge sharing and financially, and this gives me tremendous pleasure.

Andrew MacAskill: LinkedIn Top Voice: Careers | Author

Perception: Happiness is about aligning who you are with what you are doing. It is about the mindset that you bring everyday as opposed to a destination that you reach, or a single moment of joy. Sometimes when you are aligned so well, that when things go wrong it will hurt a lot more.

Impacts on happiness: There are many things which positively impact my happiness such as creativity, spending time with loved ones, moments that simply flow, progressing, growing and learning new skills. Right now, I love tennis. It is great for exercise, for developing and learning. My inner critic is a driver of my unhappiness, as well as at times I like to compare and despair, I know I shouldn't do it, but I do.

Focussing on happiness: I have experienced times of stress and so I can recognise the indicators as to when this might happen - being snappy at home, not sleeping well, diet goes south. So for me it is being alert to these and then intervening. So, I will spend time with people I care about, get into nature, reminding myself of who I am, what I have achieved.

Stories that I tell myself: I remind myself that I am a very lucky person. I do this because I feel that I am but also because I feel that lucky people attract more opportunity. I find this a great way to shut down that inner critic.

When living a happy life: For me when you are in a happy place, the rate of transmission (the R number) is very high, and that positivity can emanate onto other people. This is extremely important to me.

Jack Parsons: Co-Founder & Group CEO at *Youth Group*

Perception: Happiness is about feeling connected to both my purpose and the people around me. It's a journey, not a destination, filled with moments of growth, introspection, and genuine connections. When I'm aligned with my values and making a positive impact, that's when I feel most fulfilled and energised.

Impacts on happiness: Helping young people find their footing and thrive brings me immense joy. Every conversation, every project that contributes to their growth, is a reminder of why I do what I do. On the other hand, losing focus or straying from my values causes discontent; it's a reminder to realign and focus on what matters.

Focussing on happiness: Practising happiness is intentional. I set aside time each day for reflection, gratitude, and staying connected with those who support and inspire me. This isn't always easy, but it grounds me and gives me resilience, especially during challenging times. Staying grateful keeps me positive and fuels my commitment to those I serve.

Stories that I tell myself: Each day, I remind myself to stay true to my path and embrace progress, no matter how slow it may seem. I tell myself, "You're here for a reason, and every step counts." This helps me stay focused and resilient, even when faced with setbacks.

When living a happy life: When I'm happy and grounded, my potential feels limitless. Happiness makes me more creative, resilient, and energised to pursue my goals. It empowers me to tackle challenges with optimism and helps me connect more deeply with those around me.

Debbie Evans: Holistic Health and Wellbeing Coach

Perception: Happiness is not about the external, such as being successful in a career, having a nice car or a big house, its more meaningful that that. Happiness for me is about the internal me. It is being self-aware, aligned, balanced, content and accepting of who I am in the moment. Coupling this with finding internal joyful moments to experience and celebrate within my day provides me with my happiness.

Impacts on happiness: For me, giving something which is useful in the world, both personally and professionally, gives me a great deal of happiness. I always aim to leave people either the same or better than when I first encountered them, such as friends, work colleagues, even strangers. My yoga and meditation practices are hugely important. They help to ground me back into my body so that I don't become overwhelmed and can return to a place of balance and peace. On the flip side, injustice in the world, or if someone were to question my character would negatively impact my happiness. Additionally, I can be affected by the emotions of others, which if I am not careful, can really bring me down.

Happiness for others: It is easy to say to someone, you should do this or do that to focus on their happiness. Personally, I have always felt it's important to put the onus back onto others, so just ask yourself, are you happy with where you are? If the answer truthfully in your heart is no, then it is important to be curious to explore what is pulling on your happiness. Whether it be food relationship, not moving enough, the job you are doing, even the conversation you are having with yourself, do take a step back, reflect, ask for help and address it.

John: Spiritualist

Perception: My happiness comes from making others happy. Knowing that I have made a positive difference for them, gives me a great deal of fulfilment. If more people helped others, then it would be a better world for it.

Impacts on happiness: Sharing a joke, getting something off the shelf, changing a tyre, carrying some bags, helping people with these things gives me a lot of happiness. My work as a spiritualist, which is a huge part of my life, gives me a great deal of happiness. Using my gift to connect people, provide information, guide them, and then seeing the positive difference it makes, is the greatest reward for me. What pulls on my happiness and makes me sad, is seeing loved ones in pain, and some of what I hear that is going on in the world today.

Focussing on happiness: I have been at low spots in my life, when I have lost a job and put on a lot of weight, however what saved me was the gym. Not just the exercise and weight loss, but also the community it brings, meeting new people, which also gives me the chance to use my gift with people who need the help.

Alex Gillings: Barbour | Singer | Songwriter

Perception: My understanding of happiness is ultimately contentment. A proper relaxing of the shoulders, a confident freefall, completely trusting your surroundings, and those in it.

Impacts on happiness: My happy is often social and contagious. If the people around me are happy, or have achieved something they've wanted to for example, I really feel it for them too. I feel truly happy when I'm on stage and the crowd are completely with me. Any form of discrimination and fear makes me unhappy.

Focussing on happiness: Happiness is a key component to success. When I am unhappy, I am more creative (to write a song), but when I am happy, I am more able to sell the song. Knowing that I actively seek one or the other when needed.

Stories that I tell myself: I think of my nan and my mum, their achievements past and present, their kindness, power, tenacity and even stubbornness! Their stories inspire me, both in how to be and how not to be.

When living a happy life: I can achieve the impossible, every time. My optimism is relentless when I am happy.

Laura Duncan: Financial Analyst

Perception: I think happiness is achieved through our reaction to the things around us, rather than what those things materially are. There's joy to be found in everything if you just look for it. So, for me happiness is taking an attitude of being grateful for the things we have, and perhaps letting go of the things we don't.

Impacts on happiness: The things that make me happy are health, stability, family and friends, the beautiful country we live in (Scotland), and to have the life we do. Finally, seeing my two sons thriving makes me the happiest. In terms of what makes me unhappy, when the above are not in place.

Focussing on happiness: I try and adjust my attitude. If there's something wrong then I ask, what can I do to correct it? And if all else fails, getting outdoors for fresh air and exercise plus a good night's sleep, makes everything seem better.

Stories that I tell myself: I always think that some other people have it so much worse, and in comparison, I am very fortunate.

When living a happy life: A happy Laura can achieve way more than an unhappy Laura!

Suzie Carr: Experienced Global Human Resources Officer

Perception: Happiness is a state of pure contentment. Some people may think that word lacks excitement, not for me. For me, reaching a state of pure contentment is the best feeling in the world. It's the opposite of the endless pursuit for more - being happy with your lot. It's a feeling that brings a sense of well-being, calm, gratitude and joy.

Impacts on happiness: My husband makes me happy. Life adventures, slow mornings, a warm bed, a home, a cup of coffee, babies, dogs, laughing, friends and family, all positively impact my happiness. I can feel unhappy when life feels overwhelming, when grief is all around, and when life is unkind to those I love.

Focussing on happiness: I really work at this. I think I was born to be an optimist, glass-half-full type. Whilst I've suffered horrible loss, I always practice gratitude, not in any formal way, I just always remind myself that I have so much to be grateful for. For example, life is short and it's here for the taking, to live every day as joyful as you can, and to feel that real contentment. Do I always have it? Of course I don't. But poor me isn't something I love, and I don't like the feeling of feeling sorry for myself. So, it doesn't last long.

Stories that I tell myself: I often think of all the great opportunities I have in life. Like travel, career, the number of fantastic friends and family members I have, and the upbringing I had which was very full of love. We didn't have much money at times as a younger family, and there was a lot of grief around, but I don't think my sister or I ever really knew or noticed, because there was so much love around too. Finally, I remind myself of the love I have for my husband after twenty years together. I'm very grateful for him and what we have together. I'd choose him over and over again.

When living a happy life: A happy Suzie can achieve so much more than a lacklustre Suzie. Also, so many other things come from happiness such as energy, focus, kindness and helping others. Nothing truer than fixing your own mask first to help others.

Tony Davis Jr: Actor

My happiness reflection: For me, happiness and the growth of happiness is all about respect. Respecting that I deserve happiness, respecting those around me, and respecting the world I inhabit. True happiness grows from a world full of respecting the little things A world without respect, is a world without happiness.

Paul Fodor: COO | Chief Transformation Officer

Perception: Happiness is about balance, finding the right equation between a job you love, a family you care about, and the time you spend taking care of yourself. If any part of this equation falls apart then, for me, one can be categorised as unhappy.

Impacts on happiness: Cycling, accomplishment, recognition, food, managing my own expectations, all feed my happiness. Being told what to do and how to do it, and stress, will pull on my happiness and at times can then negatively influence how I behave.

Focussing on happiness: I faced my lowest moment in 2012. I was severely obese, smoking 20 a day, working 18-hour days, 6-7 days a week and had a heart defect. Standing by a bridge in Budapest, I said "enough is enough". From this moment I focussed on changing my fitness, my eating habits, my work life balance and medical intervention. The result, I lost 40kg, had corrective major heart surgery, can manage ten hours of exercise a week and I have stronger personal relationships. These changes and a greater focus on my happiness, have literally saved my life.

Stories that I tell myself: I remind myself of my personal achievements, despite mental health issues. Additionally, and more a learning I remind myself of, is to listen to what I and my closest think, compromising when needed. This for me is becoming increasingly liberating.

When living a happy life: Sky's the limit. In this place I am being entrepreneurial, I am free of stress, and I am supporting family.

Zoe MacAskill: LinkedIn Job Seeker Advisor | ACA Accountant

Perception: My perception of happiness is all about who I surround myself with. The positive feeling I get when being with the people who lift me, but equally in me being able to help and support them. It is about being that cheerleader for each other and I just want to make sure people are smiling. As I get older and reflect on this more, I realise that happiness for me is hugely important in my life.

Focussing on happiness: For me I like to take a multichannel approach when it comes to focussing proactively on my happiness. I spend time with my loved ones, family and friends and this gives me great joy. Of course, helping others through any context really fills my heart. Photos. I love photos, I take them daily and look at them daily, reminding me of moments, memories and experiences. Exercise also helps with my happiness. Nothing too crazy, just being active and enjoying the outdoors really makes me smile. I think this is a by-product of having lived in Melbourne!

Stories that I tell myself: There are three stand-out reminders I tell myself every day; love hard, live for today, and be kind and curious. These are super important to me. Finally, the ride of life is crazy, and for me it is especially so with a young family. At times it can get tough, however in these moments I remind myself of where we were, where we are, and where we are heading.

Nikki Berio: Mother | Director | CMO

Perception: It is accepting what life brings, living it with happiness and sharing that with others. It is about feeling good inside, laughing so hard you can't breathe, having a roof over our heads, food on the table, being satisfied in what I am doing and experiencing new things.

Impacts on happiness: I love dancing around with my kids, reading them a bedtime story, exercising and moving my body, enjoying food and wine with my husband, making other people smile, spending time with friends and family, being on a beach, and working alongside my Dad every day. Unhappiness looks like letting my family down and rude, unkind, and inconsiderate people.

Focussing on happiness: Exercise and moving my body has helped significantly with my mindset, listening to music as that instantly changes my mood, surrounding myself with good people, and ensuring I get good sleep.

Stories that I tell myself: I remind myself of how grateful I am for everything I have in life, family, friends, a job, my health, and I enjoy the small moments. I recognise that while I will get things wrong, I will learn and get stronger, it's OK to admit that we don't always have it all together.

When living a happy life: I am content, in a fun and loving environment for my children to grow, in a long and happy marriage, having a network of friends and family who love and support me, and vice versa, and I have peace with in. I can achieve anything living a happy life.

Claudia Gasson: Executive Recruiter | *Waddyado* Host

Perception: This is built around a sense of fulfilment. Strong relationships with friends and family, being healthy and physically fit, reaching career fulfilment, and challenging myself personally and professionally to achieve and learn.

Impacts on happiness: I love seeing friends and family and creating new memories with them, which is key to my mental health. Exercise and going to the gym is a key part of my every day, adventure in visiting new destinations and learning about new cultures. Music can change my mood, festivals and gigs are food for my inner self!

Focussing on happiness: Journalling not just helps me to reflect on the past, present and future, but also to read back and see how much I have learnt, grown, and achieved. It also allows me to check in on myself, see how I am feeling, and from there I often make changes to my life. Support from professionals is also very helpful including business coaches and therapists.

Stories that I tell myself: I remind myself of what I have already accomplished so to provide myself with the confidence to overcome an obstacle of fear I am presented with. I also tap into methods of cognitive behavioural therapy, whereby I outline the problem I am facing and identify a balanced argument on how I can overcome it.

When living a happy life: The world is our oyster! Happiness breeds confidence and confidence enables us to put our head to anything. Happiness coupled with resilience, focus and discipline will enable us to live a life of contentment. There will be times when life throws you off course and dark days come, but if you have the tools to find and grow your baseline happiness, then the sun will rise again.

Ant Willis: Marketplace Director | *Grind Diaries* Podcast Host

Perception: My perception of total happiness is living without restrictions. This is about not allowing my mind to hold me back because I don't believe in myself, or that I am not doing it for the right reasons. It is also not allowing my health to prevent me from enjoying life, for example walking, cycling, swimming, but also what I call "living clean". While money can't buy happiness, I want enough money put aside, so that I don't have the monetary stress of daily life.

Impacts on happiness: Seeing my family happy has the biggest impact on my happiness. Watching my son play football, my daughter laughing with friends, and my stepdaughter becoming a parent, fills my wife and I with pride and happiness. Small things can make me unhappy, someone cutting me up on a roundabout for example, but the bigger things, such as losing my job, I can work through.

Focussing on happiness: I do split this and recognise the difference between pleasure (short term) and happiness (long term). I try to build in habit and routine, allowing me to be consistent in being healthy, moving, working hard, spending time with family, but equally enjoying some beers, eating a big meal and lying in the next day.

Stories that I tell myself: I remind myself that happiness needs to be worked at daily, working long-term and building the good habits to support that. I also, using a vision board in my kitchen, to remind me of my daily standards, such as "my mind is stronger than my feelings", "discipline = freedom", and "no excuses". These act as the self-stories which are holding me to account.

When living a happy life: Is when I have purpose. Recently discovering that I have ADHD, and now at forty-two, I have discovered so much about myself and why I behaved in the way I did. Through school and in my early twenties I had no interest in what I was doing and so in turn, it brought out the worst in me. At twenty-five I found out that I would be a dad, this gave me purpose and as a result, it ignited my career and my behaviours. From this point, I have used purpose to fuel improvements in my fitness, career, living conditions, and in me as a person, for my family. Feeling and living happy gives me the belief that I am capable of anything, and in these moments, I act. A great example is last year when after a period of sustained happiness, I had the confidence to launch my podcast, *Grind Diaries*, which is now sixteen episodes old, one of which is with Jamie Mackenzie. It's ironic that I met Jamie off the back of a project that my happiness was a big driver for, and now here I am contributing to his book about happiness!

Hanna Larsson: Founder - *Huntrs* | GTM Advisor

Perception: For me this is simple, it is about freedom and being free.

Impacts on happiness: Some of my happiness drives include being free, adding value to other people, empowering others to become free, creating my own opportunities and growth, good health, and my family. If I am feeling stuck or when I let someone else define my growth and speed, then this will create unhappiness for me.

Focussing on happiness: For me, taking the decision to no longer put my own growth in the hands of an employer was a major step. Breaking free form this has been revolutionary for me, and I wish I had done it sooner.

When living a happy life: I can achieve anything, and the best part is that I am only just getting started.

Clive Hyland: Author | Neuroscience Thought Leader

Perception: My perception of happiness has changed over time, but for me at this stage of life, happiness is about the freedom. The freedom to explore and pursue the things that really matter to me.

Impacts on happiness: My family are immensely important to me, I love spending time with them, especially the grandkids. I also get great happiness from the connection that I form with other people, where I receive and offer value. Unhappiness for me comes from a sense of threat and the current state of the world, I get frustrated with this as it doesn't need to be that way.

Focussing on happiness: I consciously manage the balance of my time to ensure I am doing the things that make me happy. I create time for my own space, relationships, family, sport, fun, charity work, all these important things I proactively engage with.

Stories that I tell myself: This has come in two phases. The first, going back to my time with a focus on my corporate career, the narrative for me here was to prove myself... to me. This drove me to the success that I had. The second phase, and where I am now, was where I realised that I no longer wanted to be on that treadmill, it no longer interested me, and what I truly wanted was to give myself the permission to be free, and I remind myself of this freedom narrative every day.

Hasan Kubba: Keynote Speaker | Author | Coach

Perception: Whilst happiness is about fulfilment and contentment, for me there is a deeper sense of being about living in alignment to what I want to do and where I want to go.

Impacts on happiness: There are a few things that can promote my happiness, such as where I feel like I have been working in my flow, getting results for myself and for others too, and seeing people happy and healthy around me. It really is about a momentum and build-up of things working out. There are external factors for sure which can create unhappiness for me, but I try my best to keep those away from my inner self as much as possible.

Focussing on happiness: My happiness is very much tied to my productivity, so being an entrepreneur and driving my own business, if I am productive then that directly impacts my happiness.

Stories that I tell myself: I remind myself the story of my vision, my goals, where I am heading and the values that I want to live within me. Other stories, but more so habits, are that I want to be generous, hospitable, become more of a leader, and be a role model for my children.

Clare Bell: Property Investor

Perception: Happiness is a place and a state of mind. I can become overwhelmed with happiness when doing things, both past and present, that make me feel alive with those that I love. In gratitude I have grown to realise that everything is happy in my world when I just feel grateful.

Impacts on happiness: Heading towards my loved ones makes me happy. I travel a lot between my son and my partner, and so it's about maintaining that balance which can build solid resilience in my heart. I also love harmony, simple things, the laughter of children, and enjoying hearty food with friends. Bureaucracy, overcomplication, unfairness, unkindness, and a world that prioritises profits over people, all create unhappiness for me.

Focussing on happiness: In my younger years, I didn't give it too much airtime, I just focussed on making a mark professionally, making money, living without responsibility, being busy in life. Now in my fifties I focus on being economic with my time and energy, choosing with greater consideration than when I was younger, and using the lessons of the past to guide me.

Stories that I tell myself: I remind myself at the start of the day, the importance of being, as this makes the doing part easier, being a life and business coach, business owner, mother and human. This gives me balance, as if I get this wrong, I can end up running on reserves of anxiety, so my focus is only on the now.

When living a happy life: I can achieve anything! In calmness, in balance, in harmony and peace, nothing is beyond our reach.

Claire Hughes: Senior Leader in Higher Education

Perception: Happiness is about remembering the positives in your life and being grateful for them, not taking them for granted. It is about being mindful of grasping opportunities and turning them into something positive.

Impacts on happiness: Professionally I love to learn, I am curious, open to change, I like to innovate and be an early adopter, growing and developing people, so having these opportunities in my life every day is very important to my happiness. I love spending time with my family and being amongst nature. I believe that nature has been built purposefully to help us when we need it the most. On the flip side, I can impact my happiness negatively, it starts and ends with me, I am the maker and breaker of it.

Stories that I tell myself: I will constantly have the conversation with myself about being positive, focussing on what is going well, what is the opportunity, what can I change for a positive outcome. We have an ethos within my family, which is "aren't we lucky", whereby we try to appreciate what we have, all the time.

Tony Eames: Founder - *Total Active Hub*

Perception: For me happiness comes in two types, short-term and long-term. Having a drink with friends, going paddle boarding, buying my favourite takeaway, these are all low effort short-term happiness examples. Long-term happiness for me requires effort, challenge, risk, jeopardy, but what it leads to is self-worth, self-fulfilment, a sense of purpose.

Impacts on happiness: Striving to my goals in what I am doing is giving me happiness every day, but equally this can create friction. My family can be a distraction and a stress point on my long-term happiness, whereby there is friction in how and where I need to spend my time, sacrifices need to be made. However, I am trying my hardest to ensure that my business venture and goals, do not fail.

Focussing on happiness: Material items used to be what I did to try and make me happy, trips, nights out, cars. However, I realised that these things really didn't matter. Today I am all about movement, having a great workout, listening to music, taking time for quietness and reflection, these help me to authentically lift my happiness.

Stories that I tell myself: The first is a check-in story that I use, in it I am visualising myself playing poker and each morning when I wake up, I look at my hand, and I focus on trying to obtain better cards. The second is my story of the future, on a yacht with all the people who have helped me get to my goal, celebrating together. My final visualisation is where I am standing in a stream, no shoes on, feet cold, fighting to survive, the next minute I'm at the top of the mountain, in the sun, nice and warm – this is the most prominent one for me and represents my emotions every day.

Dion Smith: Global Leader | Board Member | Speaker

Perception: Happiness, to me, is multi-faceted and stems from balance in various areas of life. It's about finding harmony between personal fulfilment, professional success, and a sense of purpose.

Impacts on happiness: I find happiness in my family, health, financial security, and deep, meaningful relationships with friends. I love mentoring people, traveling, being active in sports, and supporting causes that resonate with my values. Unhappiness, for me, often arises when I feel that my efforts to contribute aren't making the desired impact, injustice, and professional stress that detracts from family time.

Focussing on happiness: Throughout my career, I've been deliberate in aligning my professional goals with my personal values. I've ensured that financial security and professional success never come at the expense of family or health. In the past this has meant making tough decisions. Presently, I focus on mentorship and giving back, helping others grow gives me great satisfaction.

Stories that I tell myself: I remind myself that I am in control of my happiness and success, that every challenge is an opportunity to learn, and that gratitude is key. I tell myself that each day is a new chance to make a difference, to connect meaningfully, and to improve, whether that's in my personal life or in business.

When living a happy life: I am unstoppable. I leverage my network, lead teams with inspiration, push boundaries professionally and personally, and give my time and energy back to those in need. I find with happiness comes clarity, creativity, and the ability to build deeper relationships.

Matt Phelan: Founder - *Happiness Index* | Author
Perception: Happiness, to me, is multi-faceted and stems from balance in various areas of life. For me personally it is about finding harmony between family, work and friendship.

Impacts on happiness: I find happiness in my family, health, financial security, and deep, meaningful relationships with friends. I love mentoring the next generation of entrepreneurs, travelling, being active in sports, and coaching my daughters U11s girls football team. Unhappiness, for me, often arises when I feel that my efforts to contribute aren't making the desired impact, injustice, and professional stress that detracts from family time.

Focussing on happiness: Throughout my career, I've been deliberate in aligning my professional goals with my personal values. I've worked hard so that financial security and professional success don't come at the expense of family or health although that's not always possible. In the past this has meant making tough decisions.

Stories that I tell myself: I remind myself what I can control and what I can't control when it comes to happiness and success and that every challenge or failure (of which I have many) is an opportunity to learn. I tell myself that each day is a new fresh opportunity to start over and move forward.

When living a happy life: I am always looking to learn. When I'm happier I feel a sense of balance that allows me to focus, be creative and focus on new ideas.

That was some chapter. As we reach the end of these perspectives and reflections from twenty-nine wonderful people, one thing becomes clear; there is no one size fits all version. Whilst threads of commonality run throughout, whether it's our perception of happiness, the factors that can impact it, how we choose to focus on it, or the stories that shape our direction, every individual's journey is their own. This is the magic of being human, we are all unique. Yet, within every reflection, one truth stands out, regardless of the differences, happiness is central to each person's life. I hope that through this penultimate chapter of *Sprouting Happiness – The 5 Branches to a Happy and Balanced Life*, you have found twenty-nine powerful reasons why your long-lasting happiness isn't just important, it is your priority.

Reflection moment

From the twenty-nine unique perspectives shared, which one resonated with you the most? What insights can you take from their experiences to prioritise your own long-lasting happiness?

HAPPINESS
BEGINS WITH THE COURAGE TO CHOOSE IT

Part 6:

Happily Ever After

So, here we are.

A glimpse into my soul, captured through the lens of a camera, was enough for me to truly see with clarity. With that moment came a choice. Do I continue and allow myself drift further into the depths of unhappiness, or do I summon the courage to make a change, to prioritise my happiness first and foremost, and more importantly, to stand out of my own way. I chose to move aside, and I would make the same choice again, and again.

The last sixteen months have been hard. I have stepped away from comfort zones, taken leaps of faith, confronted inherent fears, and challenged myself mind, body and soul. There were days I felt like I was moving backwards, overcome by self-doubt, anxiety, and a need for validation. Many times, I have been looking over my shoulder, tempted to cling onto the past, the comfort, the familiarity. However, each day became that little bit easier, confidence grew that little bit more, and the aura of unhappiness that once surrounded me began to fade and replaced by something brighter.

It was working.

The changes I was making were impacting me in a way I couldn't have imagined. I have never been clearer on who I am, my narrative, story, and what makes me, me. I have met some amazing people, and I am surrounded by such positivity, support and love. My relationships with those dearest to me have never felt so strong. I have a passion and an energy in me that I have never felt, I have clear mind and am in tune with my inner guide (I love you Dad). Finally, I have recognised that value is not defined by the salary you earn, but by the person you are, and I feel ten times more valuable than I did before.

I am not naive; life is not without its difficulties. However, I now face those from a baseline of long-lasting happiness which has never been so high. The five branches are embedded, and whilst they will be hit with challenges, or surrounded by the darkness of days, they will survive. And when those moments pass, light shines, opportunity comes, and the baseline will continue to grow, because I choose it.

You can choose it too.

I share this honesty with you to show that change is possible. If you take decisions and actions which are aligned with each other and are prioritising your long-lasting happiness first and foremost, then you will enjoy the fruits that come with it. For some reading this book, it might be small adjustments, for others it may well mean big decisions and big change. But change you must.

Disney created stories, fairytales, and happily ever afters. You can do the same. Use the five branches of story, people, physical, inner self and value, to help you take the first step, no matter how small, and focus on prioritising your long-lasting happiness. The rewards will be greater than you can imagine.

Thank you for joining me and twenty-nine others on this sprouting happiness journey.

Now it's your turn to write your happily ever after.

Sources:

Part 1: The Happiness Conundrum

Oxford English Dictionary: https:// www.oed.com

Cambridge Dictionary: https://dictionary.cambridge.org

Wikipedia: https://en.wikipedia.org/wiki/Happiness

Matt Phelan – Interviewed Contribution - 2024

Clive Hyland – Interviewed Contribution - 2024

2. People

Matt Phelan – Interviewed Contribution – 2024

Suzie Carr - Interviewed Contribution – 2024

3. Physical

Nikky Ricks – Interviewed Contribution – 2024

Imogen Davis – Interviewed Contribution – 2024

Tony Eames – Interviewed Contribution – 2024

Sabrina Oostberg – Interviewed Contribution – 2024

Harry Beech – Interviewed Contribution – 2024

Sleep Foundation: https://www.sleepfoundation.org

National Sleep Foundation: https://www.thensf.org

American Heart Association: https://www.heart.org

Cleveland Clinic: https://my.clevelandclinic.org

Academy of Nutrition and Dietics: https://www.eatright.org

4. Inner Self

Debbie Evans – Interviewed Contribution – 2024

John – Interviewed Contribution – 2024

Niraj Kapur – Interviewed Contribution – 2024

5. Value

Simon Alexander Ong – Interviewed Contribution – 2023

Dion Smith – Interviewed Contribution – 2024

Andrew MacAskill – Interviewed Contribution – 2024

Simon Moyle – Interviewed Contribution – 2024

Hanna Larsson – Interviewed Contribution – 2024

Ryan Hopkins – Interviewed Contribution – 2024

Hasan Kubba – Interviewed Contribution – 2024

Jack Parsons – Interviewed Contribution – 2024

Part 4: Never Give Up

Ryan Hopkins – Interviewed Contribution – 2024

Part 5: Stories Change Lives

Dion Smith – Interviewed Contribution – 2024

Andrew MacAskill – Interviewed Contribution – 2024

Simon Moyle – Interviewed Contribution – 2024

Hanna Larsson – Interviewed Contribution – 2024

Ryan Hopkins – Interviewed Contribution – 2024

Hasan Kubba – Interviewed Contribution – 2024

Jack Parsons – Interviewed Contribution – 2024

Matt Phelan – Interviewed Contribution - 2024

Clive Hyland – Interviewed Contribution - 2024

Suzie Carr - Interviewed Contribution – 2024

Nikky Ricks – Interviewed Contribution – 2024

Imogen Davis – Interviewed Contribution – 2024

Tony Eames – Interviewed Contribution – 2024

Sabrina Oostberg – Interviewed Contribution – 2024

Harry Beech – Interviewed Contribution – 2024

Debbie Evans – Interviewed Contribution – 2024

John – Interviewed Contribution – 2024

Niraj Kapur – Interviewed Contribution – 2024

Gavin Mackenzie – Interviewed Contribution – 2024

Laura Duncan – Interviewed Contribution – 2024

Ant Willis – Interviewed Contribution – 2024

Claudia Glasson – Interviewed Contribution – 2024

Tony Davis Jnr – Interviewed Contribution – 2024

Alex Gillings – Interviewed Contribution – 2024

Clare Bell – Interviewed Contribution – 2024

Zoe MacAskill – Interviewed Contribution – 2024

Paul Fodor – Interviewed Contribution – 2024

Nikki Berio – Interviewed Contribution – 2024

Claire Hughes – Interviewed Contribution - 2024

The Sprouting Happiness

Index:

Acknowledgments

I speak about gratitude, and this is my opportunity to express heartfelt thanks to everyone who has supported me in creating this very special book.

To the twenty-nine incredible individuals who generously gave their time to share their reflections, insights and advice, thank you. You have helped to shape something I know will inspire people to make positive changes in their lives. I am profoundly grateful that you trusted me with your words. You are Hanna Larsson, Andrew MacAskill, Jack Parsons, Ryan Hopkins, Matt Phelan, Simon Moyle, Clive Hyland, Debbie Evans, Dion Smith, Hasan Kubba, Tony Davies Jr, Claire Hughes, Paul Fodor, Sabrina Oostberg, Imogen Davis, Tony Eames, Nikki Berio, Niraj Kapur, Claudia Glasson, Suzie Carr, Alex Gillings, Ant Willis, Clare Bell, Zoe MacAskill, Laura Duncan, and John.

A special thank you goes to Harry Beech, Nikky Ricks, and War Machines Gym. Your support, encouragement, and the environment you've created have enabled me to achieve my goals. More than that, I feel like part of your family and am proud to call your iron paradise a home.

To Neil Summerfield, once again, you've designed something truly beautiful for this book. I will always trust your talent. You are a star, and I am deeply grateful.

Now to my inner circle. Mum, your strength and resilience through the many losses in your life is truly inspiring. Your positivity, love, and support for me and our family bring so much happiness to our lives. Thank you, I love you.

Teddy, you make me smile so much. Your energy and honesty have been invaluable throughout this writing journey. Thank you for keeping me on track. You are so much more than "just a waitress."

To my wife, Nicola: you listened to me, supported me, and gave me the energy I needed to change. You continue to encourage me to pursue what I love and believe in. I will always be grateful for the happiness you bring to my life every single day.

To my boys, Leo and Cameron, you bring me happiness every day. Your energy and togetherness remind me of another pair of brothers who will always be there for each other. I can't wait to keep playing football with you both, and this time, for as long as you want.

My brother Gavin, it's hard to find the right words to express my gratitude for all you've done these last few months. In short, you've helped me change my health and life for the better. You have been the cornerstone of my happiness for the last 40 years, and every today and tomorrow are brighter because you're with me.

I must also mention my dad, my inner guide, who I know watches over me every day, keeping me on the right path. And to my nan, Mopsie, who sadly passed away this year. You were one of my biggest advocates and supporters and I dedicate this book to you and hope you look on with pride.

Finally, thank you to you, the reader, for investing your time and money in this book. I hope you've enjoyed it and that it has inspired you to prioritise your long-lasting happiness.

About The Author:

Jamie Mackenzie

With over two decades of leadership experience in multinational corporations and a lifetime of personal transformation, Jamie has discovered the profound impact of storytelling on communication, connection, and change. His journey from corporate boardrooms to becoming a bestselling author, speaker, coach, and social entrepreneur is rooted in one powerful truth: Stories Change Lives.

Jamie's mission is to inspire people of all ages to harness the power of storytelling to create meaningful connections, drive positive change, and prioritise long-lasting happiness. Through his work, Jamie equips individuals, teams, and organisations with tools that transform how they communicate and inspire action.

Whether you're engaging with Jamie as a reader, participant, or partner, you'll discover how stories can shape perspectives, strengthen relationships, empower growth, and make life changing impacts.

Based by the seaside in Kent, Jamie treasures creating new memories with his family, moments that remind him every day of the beauty and power of the stories we live and share.

Explore More Books from Jamie

SPROUTING HAPPINESS
THE JOURNAL

Inspired by the book, Sprouting Happiness – The 5 Branches to a Happy and Balanced Life, this essential companion features prompts and space centred around the five branches. It allows you to track progress, reflect deeply, and stay motivated as you move forward in prioritising your long-lasting happiness.

available at

amazon

28 BAGS OF SPROUTS

STORYTELLING WITH IMPACT

Storytelling is the fabric of all communication connecting eight billion people across the world... and you can harness its power. Join Jamie, supported by six expert contributors, as he coaches you through the sprout model, a unique storytelling approach that will unlock a superpower in you.

available at

180

Share and Connect

Don't forget to leave a review for the book, and share with your friends, family and network, how it is helping you to prioritise your long-lasting happiness.

Stories. Change. Lives.

Connect with Jamie who would love to hear about how you are sprouting your happiness and the positive impact it is making.

(Email) jamie@jamie-mackenzie.com

(Instagram) @jamie.r.mackenzie

(Facebook) @jamie mackenzie

(LinkedIn) @jamiermackenzie

(X) @jamiermackenzie

(TikTok) @jamiermackenzie

(YouTube) @jamie-mackenzie

www.jamie-mackenzie.com

#sproutinghappiness

Let's share.

Printed in Great Britain
by Amazon

55164989R00111